The Team Building Tool Kit

Tips, Tactics, and Rules for Effective Workplace Teams

Deborah Harrington-Mackin

amacom
American Management Association
New York • Atlanta • Boston • Chicago • Kansas City • San Francisco • Washington, D.C.
Brussels • Toronto • Mexico City

This book is available at a special discount when ordered in bulk quantities. For information, contact Special Sales Department, AMACOM, a division of American Management Association, 135 West 50th Street, New York, NY 10020.

This publication is designed to provide accurate and authoritative information in regard to the subject matter covered. It is sold with the understanding that the publisher is not engaged in rendering legal, accounting, or other professional service. If legal advice or other expert assistance is required, the services of a competent professional person should be sought.

Library of Congress Cataloging-in-Publication Data

Harrington-Mackin, Deborah.
The team building tool kit : tips, tactics, and rules for effective workplace teams / Deborah Harrington-Mackin.
p. cm.
Includes bibliographical references and index.
ISBN 0-8144-7826-3 :
1. Work groups. 2. Interpersonal relations. 3. Organizational effectiveness. I. Title.
HD60.H387 1994
658.4'02—dc20 *93-24834*
CIP

Printing number

10 9 8 7 6 5 4 3 2 1

Contents

Acknowledgments

Our work with teams began six years ago when we were asked to create the training modules for a jointly owned Japanese-American manufacturing company. The original team leaders and the first group of employees came from traditional work environments. They had to work just as hard on issues of trust and communication as on team structure and tasks.

Since then, we have helped many companies and nonprofit organizations design, train, and implement all types of teams, from organizational decision-making teams to self-directed and cross-functional teams.

Our special thanks to the teams at Hemmings Motor News, Nastech Manufacturing, Moore Business Forms, Bijur Lubricating Corporation, North Adams Regional Hospital, Northshire Bookstore, Mother Myrick's Confectionery and Ice Cream Parlor, Southwest Vermont Supervisory Union, Southwest Vermont Career Development Center, Bennington College, Shaftsbury Vermont School Climate Team, Pfizer/Specialty Minerals, Inc., Eveready Battery, Stanley Tools, and Storey Communications for their contributions during training sessions, which aided in the development of this material.

A very special note of gratitude to the staff of New Directions Management Services: to longtime employee and friend Lisa Dunbar, for her research and editing skills; to Forrest Green, for his suggestions and support; to Sue Toussaint, for finding our publisher; and, most important, to Susan Bernier, for her desktop publishing skills, artful design work, and patience in reworking the material. I would also like to thank Dawn Raphan-Lee and Kat Farnham, who helped with editing.

On a more personal side, I thank my family—my husband Paul and our children Michael, Sarah, Andrew, Matthew, Ben, and Molly—for the effort they give every day to our own blended team.

Introduction

Several years ago a team was in the process of drafting a set of rules to govern member behavior, team meetings, team structure, and even the smaller issues such as how to orient new members. Many hours were spent researching books and articles about teams, with members becoming increasingly frustrated at the length of time it was taking to come up with anything specific and helpful.

The Team Building Tool Kit was created to be that single resource for start-up and existing teams as they develop their rules. The format follows the life cycle of a team: Getting Started, Team Meetings, Team Behavior, Problems of Fear and Control, Team Decision Making and Problem Solving, Evaluating and Rewarding Team Performance, and Training.

This book was written for all types of teams, from multifunctional to self-managed, in both profit-making and nonprofit organizations. In addition, trainers and college faculty will find it a valuable reference for teaching team building skills to others.

The book can be used in a variety of ways. The layout is designed to make it an easy reference tool, even in the middle of a team meeting when a question arises (e.g., "how do we want to handle confidentiality issues?"). It can be read cover to cover, a particularly good approach for someone unfamiliar with how to get teams started. Certain sections, such as Chapter 4, which discusses fear and control, can be read by team members to help them achieve a common level of understanding before discussing these issues as an entire group.

The question-and-answer sections at the ends of the chapters are designed to supplement the chapter material with real-life situations. (Within each chapter, there are highlighted references in the margins to specific questions in the question-and-answer section that pertain to the text at hand. These references provide a quick, handy way to find the question and answer that correlates to the topic being discussed.) We've included typical questions asked of us as we've helped teams get started and mature.

The Nature of Teams

It is important to keep in mind that a team is a means to an end—an approach for achieving a goal, whether that goal is improved production, increased quality, better morale, or happier customers.

Each team has one thing in common: the need for rules to govern itself. Rules play a crucial role in the team's success:

- Rules are usually determined in the early months of a team's development, and, once established, they are difficult to modify or revise.
- Any changes in team rules require substantial time and often cause team members to get upset.
- The team leader plays an important part in the setting of rules; what the leader doesn't do can be as important as what the leader does do.
- Commitment to behavior boundaries is strongest in small teams.
- Teams usually judge their members by how closely they conform to the rules; members who most closely conform to the rules earn the greatest respect.
- The more team members work together to develop team rules, the more they will agree with each other.
- A team willing to create rules is a team willing to be self-disciplined and to assume responsibility for its behavior.
- When a team is not clear about its rules, it often lacks control over its members.
- Rules help to equalize the power of all members.

Many organizations are creating teams. When the team building is done poorly, the teams are viewed as an end in and of themselves, and little money or effort is invested to help them be successful. Such teams usually last about six months. They make little difference to the company other than to allow it to use the word "team" to describe their internal structure, and the team members are actually more frustrated than they were before the teams were created.

Successful teams, on the other hand, are viewed as a strategy—a synergistic blending of human resources—for achieving an organization's goals. Money, effort, and, most important, patience and support are invested eagerly. There is strong recognition that operating as a team is different from what we are used to from our experiences at school and at home and that, in order to be successful, we need to learn how to play by new rules.

A Brief History of Team Building

18th and 19th century. Before the industrial movement began, work was conducted in small groups consisting of a master craftsman and a group of apprentices. The master functioned as the teacher, carefully instructing the apprentices in a trade. After many years of training, apprentices were able to determine and improve their own work.

1924. Elton Mayo, founder of the human relations movement, conducted research at the Hawthorne works of Western Electric Company. His study confirmed the relationship between human factors, such as self-respect, recognition, and self-direction, and productivity (Mayo, 1933).

1930s. Kurt Lewin researched the aspect of team behavior known as group dynamics and developed a tool called Force Field Analysis to improve team effectiveness (Lewin, 1951).

1940s. Britain's Tavistock Institute documented that productivity increases when workers are organized into teams.

Abraham Maslow defined his hierarchy of needs, linking motivation and performance (Maslow, 1943).

1950s. General Foods experimented with self-directed work teams in its Topeka, Kansas, plant. The experiment was successful but was not regarded favorably by traditional organizations (Lawler, 1986).

Sensitivity groups (also known as T-groups) were studied; these were highly unstructured groups in which members shared feelings and offered feedback to one another. The groups required supervision to ensure that they did not drift off into unproductive activities (Lewin, 1951).

Toyota's production chief, Taiichi Ohno, studied Ford's factories and developed the Toyota production system, a team model for quality and efficiency.

1960s. Douglas McGregor listed the characteristics of effective teams and of the leadership styles known as Theory X and Y (McGregor, 1960).

Two members of the Tavistock Institute, Trist and Bamforth (1951), conducted a study demonstrating the impact of teams and organizational change (reported in Glaser, 1991). A British mining company had introduced a new technique for coal mining called the longwall method, which replaced miners with machines and spread the workflow over three shifts to resemble a factory assembly line.

Under the old method, mining was conducted in teams of three men: a hewer, a mate, and an assistant using the "hand-got method." The team was responsible for removing the coal from the face of the mine and for working together to complete all the tasks. The process demanded close working relationships that often spilled over into the miners' personal lives. Traditional supervision was neither necessary nor desired.

When the new longwall method was implemented, absenteeism increased and productivity decreased. Trist and Bamforth found that the company had disregarded the importance of the miners' team relationships and the impact of these relationships on morale and productivity.

Trist and Bamforth were able to show the company how it could enjoy the benefits of technological advances while allowing the miners to maintain the social relationships that were so important to them, without returning to the "hand-got method." This early research demonstrated the importance of maintaining a balance between established social patterns and technological change in the workplace.

Chris Argyris defined the interpersonal behaviors required of effective team members (1964).

The quality of worklife movement began in the United States as managers asked employees for ideas that would make their jobs easier and more pleasant.

General Motors discovered that team-based assembly operations established in conjunction with production-line operations resulted in a much higher quality of product and greater job satisfaction without increasing the time required to produce a car.

1970s. In Sweden, Saab and Volvo established work assembly teams and built a new plant in which cars were ferried to different teams of workers. The new system resulted in improved morale and a 25 percent reduction in production costs (Hunsaker and Curtis, 1986).

Quality circles (QCs) began to take hold in the United States as a way to improve quality and cut costs.

In Japan, five million workers belonged to QCs by 1972.

A joint venture between Toyota and General Motors achieved outstanding quality and productivity levels with its New United Motor Manufacturing, Inc. (NUMMI) teams (Lee, 1988).

1980s. Honeywell assigned all plant functions to teams (Chance, 1989).

Xerox supported team problem solving by encouraging teams to form a "huddle" twice daily (Industrial Relations News, 1981).

Cheseborough-Ponds used a high-intensity task force to reposition products (Feder and Mitchell, 1988).

Pratt and Whitney established special teams as part of its effort to increase production capability (Herman and Herman, 1989).

Volvo traded the traditional assembly line for self-managed teams of seven to ten employees.

Westinghouse Furniture Systems teams increased productivity by 74 percent in three years (Hoerr, 1987).

Volvo's innovative Kalmar facility teams in Sweden reduced defects by 90 percent (Patinkin, 1987).

AAL increased productivity by 20 percent, cut personnel by 10 percent, and handled 10 percent more transactions (Hoerr, 1989).

Shenandoah Life Insurance Company in Roanoke, Virginia,

reduced staffing needs and increased work volume by 33 percent, creating a $200,000 savings per year (O'Dell, 1989).

General Electric Company's Salisbury, North Carolina, plant increased productivity by 250 percent (Hoerr, 1989).

1990s. Florida Power and Light has 1,900 quality teams, and nearly every employee participates in a team.

Xerox has more than seven thousand quality improvement teams involving about 75 percent of all employees.

A one-year pilot suggestion program designed by a team of Citizens Gas and Coke employees results in the implementation of more recommendations than had taken place over the previous thirty-four years combined.

An *Industry Week* study shows that one-fourth of organizations in North America are experimenting with self-directed work teams.

Teams at Federal Express Corporation cut service errors by 13 percent (Dumaine, 1990).

Carrier, a division of United Technologies Corporation, reduces turnaround time for units in its team-based Georgia facility from two weeks to two days (Wysocki, 1990).

Corning's new specialty cellular ceramics plant decreases defect rates from 1,800 parts per million to nine parts per million through team effort (Sheridan, 1990).

General Mills finds that plants that use teams are as much as 40 percent more productive than plants operating without teams (Dumaine, 1990).

AT&T's Richmond, Virginia, operator service team increases service quality by 12 percent (Wesner and Egan, 1990).

Dana Corporation's Minneapolis valve plant reduces customer lead time from six months to six weeks by using teams (Sheridan, 1990).

Teams have a two-hundred-year history to draw upon for valuable information. Short-lived teams—and yes, there are some—think team building is no more than getting along together. In reality, effective teams build on the vast experiences of others to challenge their members to change their behaviors to accommodate the needs of the team.

Chapter 1
Getting Started

The most successful teams have strong upper management support, demonstrated partly by the CEO's commitment to the team process and expressed confidence that success is achievable. Team building begins with a decision at the top to encourage, and even to require, employees to operate in teams. Lack of management support is the number one cause of team failure.

Management Commitment

Management at all levels must support team efforts openly and without reservation if it expects teams to succeed. Yet managers and supervisors sometimes feel threatened and may even take credit away from the team when improvements are made. They often fail to realize that their own involvement in team activities will promote trust and cooperation between them and their subordinates and will enhance their own reputation as effective managers.[1]

Typically, we have seen newly formed teams look to upper management over and over to test the organization's commitment to team building. Managers must take special care to reiterate their belief in the team's future and to check critical offhand remarks or statements of frustration.

Before proceeding, management must be aware of the benefits and the drawbacks of teams.

Key Benefits of Teams

- Highly motivated environment; better work climate
- Shared ownership and responsibility for tasks
- Faster response to technological change
- Fewer, simpler job classifications
- Better response to the less formal values of a younger generation of employees
- Effective delegation of work load; increased flexibility in task assignments
- Common commitment to goals and values; complete buy-in
- Proactive approach to problems; innovative and effective problem solving
- Improved self-worth
- Increased communication
- Better decisions
- Skill development of staff; cross-training in roles and responsibilities
- Early warning system for problems

Key Drawbacks

- Can be time-consuming; sometimes do not leave enough time for regular work
- Appear confused, disorderly, and out of control
- Can cause role confusion; members have difficulty leaving "hats" at the door
- Are viewed negatively by "old school" people who like order and control
- Require a long time (three to five years) to produce results
- Require people to change

Researchers have found that the effectiveness of teams is greatly influenced by members' attitudes about the organization. If the team members feel support and commitment from management, they will exhibit high productivity. If team members are angry because of a lack of organizational support, they will limit their efforts.[2]

Types of Teams

As an organization begins its team building efforts, one of the first concerns it must resolve is what types of teams to create.

The green light for team building is typically a top-management decision. Some organizations begin with high-level policy-making teams charged with identifying broad concerns and setting goals, whereas others begin with small departmental teams. Whether the impetus comes from a companywide policy review or from a departmental task force, teams should be formed only when an achievable goal with a specific objective can be identified.

The variety of teams is somewhat like a flower garden: All serve a particular purpose and have their own characteristics and sets of benefits.

Organizational Policy-Making Teams (Multifunctional)

- Identify major areas of concern/opportunity; articulate organizational needs
- Develop philosophy, policies, and direction
- Establish goals and objectives
- Formulate implementation plans
- Identify resources needed to achieve goals
- Monitor progress, measure and report results; establish time lines and completion target dates
- Include members from every level of the organization
- Require long meetings and meet over extended periods of time
- Are sometimes called Quality Councils
- Can function as organization's management team if so empowered

Task-Force or Cross-Functional Teams

- Include between five and eight members; membership based on experience
- Comprise individuals from two or more different work areas
- Necessitate long meetings over a short period of time

- Implement strategic plan for addressing problem/concern/opportunity; others may complete the implementation of the plan
- Assume investigative, corrective, interactive function
- Are sometimes called Process Improvement Teams or Product Launch Teams

Department Improvement Teams (Functional)

- Include only department members
- Select problems; identify solutions
- Restrict scope of activity to within department
- Have short meetings that extend over a long period of time

Quality Circles

- Include members from functional areas who work together on specific quality, productivity, and service problems
- Are voluntary in nature
- Select problem; may not have power and authority to transform ideas into action
- Receive minimal management direction; manager may be left with responsibility for implementation
- Are often temporary
- Serve as forerunner of self-directed work teams

Self-Directed Work Teams (Functional)

- Comprise an intact team of employees who work together on an ongoing, day-to-day basis and who are responsible for a "whole" work process or segment
- Assume "ownership" of product or service and are empowered to share various management and leadership functions
- Are limited to a particular work unit
- Function semiautonomously; are responsible for controlling the physical and functional boundaries of their work and for delivering a specified quantity and quality of a product or service within a specified time and at a defined cost

- Are all cross-trained in a variety of work skills
- Share and rotate leadership responsibilities; team members have equal input in decisions
- Accept the concept of multiskills and job rotation (except for jobs requiring years of training and technical expertise)
- Work together to improve operations, handle day-to-day problems, and plan and control work
- Set own goals and inspect own work; often create own work and vacation schedules and review performance as a team
- May prepare own budgets and coordinate work with other departments
- Usually order materials, keep inventories, and deal with suppliers
- Are frequently responsible for acquiring new training and maintaining on-the-job training
- May hire own replacements and assume responsibility for disciplining own members
- Monitor and review overall process performance

Most self-directed work teams gradually take on responsibility for these tasks as they gain confidence in their own skills and are able to redefine the role of the supervisor. The shift to self-direction represents change, and with change comes resistance.

Self-Managed Teams (Functional)

- Operate with varying degrees of authority and without a visible manager
- Contract with management to assume management responsibility in addition to performing its specific jobs, including planning, organizing, directing, and monitoring
- Learn and share jobs usually performed by a manager
- Control own operation
- Often report in a "skip-level" pattern to managers two or more levels above them who act as integrators/facilitators; may report to "absentee" manager away on special assignment or to a manager with broad responsibility managing several functions[3]

- Hold weekly team meetings
- Identify own goals and team direction
- Persuade others in organization to accept team's goals
- Schedule and coordinate daily and occasional tasks of the team and individuals
- Design and conduct cross-training on all tasks
- Set performance standards for the work team
- Screen applicants and interview job candidates for the team
- Hire or make hiring recommendations
- Provide orientation for new team members
- Coach and provide feedback on member performance
- Conduct new team member's evaluations during probationary period
- Plan and adopt a budget
- Collect performance data; review results
- Meet requests from inside and outside the team
- Identify, analyze, and solve task and relationship problems

The Basics of Team Functioning

Forming a Team

The first step in forming a team is to define a goal for the team on the basis of the subject or problem to be examined. An expected deadline, interim steps, and key questions to be answered are also specified.

In some cases, the team will have to define its own goal. Although there is nothing wrong with this approach, having the team establish its own goal means that the team will take longer to get started on specific tasks than if a design team or steering committee had determined the initial goal.

Getting Started on Team Building

Q&A #1

- Describe key activities the team is expected to undertake, including specific objectives to be achieved or strategies, recommendations, or analyses to be performed. Require a

work plan, charts, reports, and presentations, if necessary.
- Identify the results expected of the team, such as improvements, savings, gains, and benefits.
- Identify the resources available to the team, including the team adviser, subject matter expert (SME), or single point of contact (SPOC). (Definitions are given later in this chapter.)
- Identify the type and frequency of reporting and the communication expected of the team, including who should receive copies of the team minutes and any interim reports.
- Identify any nonnegotiable requirements or rules the team is expected to adhere to or that it needs to be aware of.
- Identify the skills and abilities necessary for the team to accomplish its task.
- Identify the authority level the team will have—what decisions it may or may not make and any spending limitations.
- Identify the owners' roles and responsibilities (if applicable).
- Select a core team to build the first meeting agenda and to identify the first step. Select an interim facilitator for the first meeting.

Figure 1-1 provides a form for you to write in the information listed above.

Determining Level of Authority

When a team is created to perform a specific task or to deal with a specific issue, it should be assigned a clear level of authority, defining the limits within which it may act autonomously.

Authority Options

- Look into the problem and provide all the details; others will decide what to do.
- Identify the alternatives available and the pros and cons of each; others will decide which to select. Q&A #4
- Recommend a course of action for others' approval.

Figure 1-1. Forming a team outline.

____
Name of Team

1. Team Goal ____

2. Expected Activities ________________________________

3. Expected Results __________________________________

4. Resources Available _______________________________

5. Communication ____________________________________

6. Nonnegotiables ____________________________________

7. Skills/Qualities Necessary ___________________________

8. Other Important Criteria ____________________________

9. Team Membership ___________________________________

10. Invitation/Background Recommendation __________________

11. Other ____

- Report what the team intends to do; delay action until approval is received.
- Report what the team intends to do; do it unless told not to.
- Take action; report action; report results.
- Take action; communicate only if the action is unsuccessful.
- Take action; no further communication is necessary.

Even in traditional management structures, decision-making authority is often not clear. In the excitement of getting started, teams sometimes give themselves more authority than they truly have. Later, when the presumed authority is clarified (and more limited), the team experiences great disappointment. It's wise to place clear limits on the team right at the start.

Establishing Team Membership

A team can comprise a complete working unit (functional teams) or can include people from throughout the organization, including hourly staff and top management.

Whenever possible, it is best to seek volunteers for team members. People required to be on teams often lack commitment to the team process and act to undermine the team's progress.

The critical issue that surfaces with team membership is inclusion and exclusion—who is or isn't on a team. Members on a team begin to flaunt their special status; employees not on teams are often left behind to "do the real work," and resentment grows.

When in doubt, it is better to include people on teams than to exclude them.

If there are no volunteers or staff to fill a vacancy, the team must look for another solution. It is not beneficial to leave positions vacant for long periods of time unless team members agree to do so.

There are favorable and unfavorable times to introduce new members on a team. Generally, a team that is experiencing problems or has suddenly entered into a new phase of development will not readily welcome a new member; if problems exist, members may use the new member to avoid confronting them.[4]

The larger the percentage of new members on an existing team, the more resistance there will be to their inclusion. For best team functioning, a minimal amount of training should be required of all team members in areas such as interpersonal skills, leadership skills, and problem-solving skills (see Chapter 7, which discusses team training).

Determining Optimal Team Size

If the team's goals and tasks are complex and demand considerable skill, small teams (from six to twelve members) are most effective. If tasks are relatively simple and redundant, teams can be sufficiently large to provide something meaningful to manage. If the team is responsible for a task requiring a lot of technological know-how, the team size should be large enough to include people who can perform the job, as well as those who can manage—and even design—the product (a cross-functional team).

The decision about team size must be based in part on how willing members are to help the team function smoothly. Members of a large team (between fifteen and twenty-five members) have to be mature enough not to speak on every issue and to be willing to delegate certain tasks to subgroups.

Orienting New Members

Orientation of new members is the responsibility of the team, not the new member.

To shorten the start-up time for a new member, make sure he or she is properly oriented to the team, its members, and its work to date. Orientation should occur within thirty days of placement on a team and should include:

- An overview of training specific to that team
- A review of the team's history and its purpose in forming
- A review of team minutes, with an emphasis on decisions made to date
- The sharing of all pertinent information and data

- A discussion of roles and responsibilities agreed to by the team

One way to orient new members is to have them interview three or four people on the team for specific information. Another option is to have the new member work one on one with a senior team member.

Using Member Substitutions

A substitute is a person who sits in for a team member when he or she is unable to attend a team meeting. Substitutes are used when members sit on several teams and have occasional scheduling conflicts.

Each team decides when and where substitutions are appropriate. Generally, substitution should be voluntary, and equality and fairness of opportunity should be taken into consideration in choosing substitutes. Substitutes should receive an agenda and an update on items to be discussed.

Implementing a "buddy" system also helps to keep members and substitutes current about team projects. Each team member is a buddy to another team member and is responsible for collecting materials and informing the member of any decisions made in his or her absence.

Removing a Member From the Team

Removing a member from a team is an act of tremendous significance for both the member and the team. When a person is asked to leave or chooses to leave a team, it is up to the team to handle the situation as effectively as possible.

Once the team has determined that a team member is not working effectively, a procedure that basically follows these steps has proved to work with most teams.

Steps for Removing a Team Member

1. The team leader and the two process observers (see page 17) meet with the difficult team member and identify the

behavior that is causing problems. They remind the team member of his or her agreement to support the help/hinder list (see Figure 1-2), which defines acceptable and unacceptable behaviors in the team, and seek commitment from the member to change.
2. If the member refuses, the team leader and process observers bring the result of the meeting back to the team for discussion. A consensus decision by the team is required to remove a member.
3. The team leader or someone designated by the team meets with the difficult member and reports the team's decision. Research has shown that it is not particularly helpful to invite the member back for a final meeting to try to work things through.

When a person is removed from the team, it's important to expect a powerful reaction from the rest of the team. The ejection of a team member stirs up deep levels of anxiety associated with the need for approval and belonging.

Handling Resignation Requests

In the normal course of events, teams can expect to lose up to 30 percent of their members in the first year. Resignation requests should be presented to the team in writing.

Whenever a resignation occurs, every effort should be made by the team to conduct an exit interview to determine why the member has resigned.

Conducting an Exit Interview

If the resignation is accepted, an exit interview conducted by several members of the team is required, and a summary report of the interview must go back to the full team.

Questions Included in the Exit Interview

- Why did you decide to leave the team?
- How did the process work for you?

Figure 1-2. Sample help/hinder list.

Behaviors in the Team That . . .

Help	*Hinder*
Be on time/be prepared	Be critical, negative
Participate, volunteer	Attack personality
Engage in open, honest communication	Dominate
Listen to understand; speak to be understood	Engage in name calling/ stereotyping
Stick to the agenda	Be manipulative
Build on others' ideas	Jump from one topic to another
Be optimistic/positive about team	Mask statements as questions
Criticize ideas, not members	Selectively interpret
Provide leadership (when needed) without threatening formal facilitator	Agree with everything
Perform promised follow-up	Avoid decision making or closure through sarcasm
Pay attention, stay open-minded	Seek sympathy
Take problems seriously	Express futility, resignation, or helplessness
Be courteous, honest, trusting	Withdraw psychologically
Say what you feel/think	Reflect boredom/don't pay attention
Take risks	Be prejudiced
Use "we" expressions and thought	Be close-minded
Support each other	Use "you" statements
Show commitment toward making it work	Don't communicate, cooperate, or participate
Display a sense of humor	Judge ideas/others
Set realistic goals/time frame on goals	Don't listen (engage in subconversations)
Establish clearly defined roles	Do other distracting work
Distribute labor equally	

- What needs improvement (structure, communication, conflict resolution)?
- What should stay the same?
- Did you feel you had adequate training?
- Did you feel you had support from the team?
- What would you change about the way the team approaches tasks?
- What would you change in the team's approach to relationships?
- Are there concerns that you were uncomfortable discussing in the team that you are willing to discuss now?
- Are there any loose ends still to be resolved at this time?
- If circumstances change, would you consider returning to the team? Why or why not?

Most team members disguise the reasons they are leaving the team in order to preserve their relationships. Even so, it's important for team members to try to surface problems and hidden conflicts. Sometimes a close friend or two can get the individual to discuss the real issues.

Assigning Team Roles

Team roles should be assigned and/or clarified at the beginning of each team meeting.

A healthy team allows members to be flexible in their roles. This flexibility may be encouraged by rotating duties and responsibilities.

Q&A #10

*Responsibilities of Supervisor**

- Transmits information, knowledge, and skills, in a timely fashion to team members
- Interprets and applies policies, work specifications, and job orders for the team
- Teaches team members how to manage work processes effectively and to evaluate results

*Sometimes called Coordinator or Team Leader.

- Builds communication channels between departments and eliminates duplication of effort
- Encourages team to identify what can be done differently or better
- Models proper team behavior in all areas; helps establish team climate and shape attitudes
- Promotes self-discipline in team members
- Encourages risk taking among team members by confronting groupthink
- Supports goals of the team to internal and external customers
- Reinforces and rewards proper team behavior
- Troubleshoots for the team in areas of expertise
- Communicates team progress to management
- Serves as a mediator during team conflicts to create win/win resolution
- Guides and shapes the direction toward a team culture

Supervisors have the greatest role change during the transition to teams, and most need training to gain confidence in the new role. Management plays an important role here, helping the supervisor cope with the loss of power and control.

Responsibilities of Team Adviser*

- Develops and communicates the team's purpose so that it is clearly understood by all members
- Provides hands-on assistance in the beginning, pulling back as the team matures
- Assists team facilitator and process observers by keeping them aware of intradepartmental considerations
- Helps to resolve team conflicts
- Reviews team goals to ensure they are achievable and challenging enough to meet organizational needs
- Helps obtain the cooperation and support required to achieve team goals
- Follows the progress of the team's accomplishments; rein-

*Sometimes called Quality Coordinator, Team Manager, or Team Developer.

forces achievement and assists in problem solving when necessary
- Identifies resources needed (people, time, money, materials, facilities) and ensures they are available
- Determines performance standards and how results will be measured

Responsibilities of Facilitator

- Schedules, arranges, and conducts the meeting
- Prepares and distributes agenda before the meeting and ensures that agenda is followed during the meeting
- Clarifies purpose and helps the team identify goals
- Ensures that all team functions are assigned to various team members
- Encourages everyone to participate throughout the discussion
- Summarizes and organizes the ideas discussed to gain commitment
- Identifies common topics or subjects in discussion to maintain direction of discussion
- Asks questions to clarify comments and restates if members are confused
- Tests for consensus by stating the position that appears to be the team's conclusion
- Assists members in dealing with team conflicts in a productive manner
- Joins process observers in pointing out feelings that are interfering with team's work
- Helps team sort out areas of agreement from areas of disagreement
- Models performance standards, active listening, and trust-building behaviors
- Instills accountability in all team members
- Keeps team adviser and supervisor apprised of progress on a regular basis
- Protects the right of team members to have and to express different points of view
- Encourages team to finish each agenda item before moving on to the next

- Serves as person known to all; interacts within and outside the organization

Key Components in Productive Teams

Productive teams often display the following characteristics:

- Team goals are as important as individual goals; members are able to recognize when a personal agenda is interfering with the team's direction.
- The team understands the goals and is committed to achieving them; everyone is willing to shift responsibilities.
- The team climate is comfortable and informal; people feel empowered; individual competitiveness is inappropriate.
- Communication is spontaneous and shared among all members; diversity of opinions and ideas are encouraged.
- Respect, open-mindedness, and collaboration are high; members seek win/win solutions and build on each others' ideas.
- Trust replaces fear, and people feel comfortable taking risks; direct eye contact and spontaneous expression are present.
- Conflicts and differences of opinion are considered opportunities to explore new ideas; the emphasis is on finding common ground.
- The team works on improving itself constantly by examining its procedures, processes, and practices, and experimenting with change.
- Leadership is rotated; no one person dominates.
- Decisions are made by consensus and have the acceptance and support of members.

Causes of Team Failure

Some organizations believe they can implement teams without changing the traditional hierarchical structure. Within months the two structures inevitably clash. Typically the more entrenched structure survives, and teamwork is reduced to a thing of the past.

The most common reasons for a team's failure include the following:

- Its structure is incompatible with hierarchial organizational structure.
- It lacks visible support and commitment from top management.
- It has focused on task activities to the exclusion of work on team member relationships.
- Its members lack self-discipline and are unwilling to take responsibility for their own behavior and actions.
- The team has too many members and lacks the strong structure necessary to deal with a large team.
- Team members are unwilling to recognize and accept the patterns and stages of team process.
- The team has experienced poor leadership within and/or outside the team; there has been resistance from first-line supervisors.
- The organization has failed to use team efforts in any meaningful way.
- Members have received insufficient training.

Closing Out a Team

When a team has completed its purpose, it is important to provide closure for the members. This is a time to reflect on progress and to celebrate the team's accomplishments. Here is a sample process for making the closure effective:

1. Schedule a meeting to present the team's findings and recommendations.
2. Invite anyone affected by the team's recommendations.
3. Decide on a review procedure and a completion date for assessing the team's recommendations.
4. Recognize and reward the team's accomplishments in

some formal manner (see Chapter 6 for a discussion of how to reward a team's accomplishments).

5. Identify any other areas of the organization that could benefit from the team's ideas or skills.

Here are some additional points on closure:

- Share stories about what it was like working on the team.
- Identify key skills learned.
- Develop tips for other teams.
- Determine how improvements will be maintained.
- Complete all documentation and final reports.
- Decide on a way to say good-bye.

Questions and Answers: Starting and Building Teams

1. **Q.** *Where do we begin the team building process? Do we start with the whole organization or choose a specific department? If we choose a department, do we select one that is weak or strong?*

A. Although organizations begin at various places in the team building process, for best results start with an internal climate analysis: a set of questions that all employees are asked to complete on their perceptions of the organization, its management, systems, and structures. The results of the confidential questionnaires are tabulated into a final summary that immediately identifies the organization's strengths and weaknesses as perceived by those within the organization.

After the results are shared with employees, decisions can be made about where teams might be most effective. For example, the climate analysis may show that policies and procedures are weak. The organization can then form a cross-functional team to work on the problem. The climate analysis may show that results are lower than acceptable in a particular department where management skill is weak.

People may decide to form a self-directed work team in the department to compensate for specific weaknesses.

We have seen no significant difference between starting with a strong or weak department, because both will need to learn a very new and different set of skills.

2. **Q.** *How much information should we share with team members about the business and what should we keep private?*

A. This question upsets many business owners and managers who believe that information about the business—especially financial information—should not be shared.

We believe that team members must have access to whatever information they need to make wise decisions. The organization's leaders cannot withhold important information and then blame a team for making a foolish choice.

We have seen no situation in which team members have violated the confidentiality of a business's information, whether related to finance, product development, or customer base, if requested to keep it private. In fact, most employees take less risk than owners do. For example, in an organization that was deciding whether to purchase a new building, we heard reports of team members who refused to discuss anything about negotiations even with their spouses.

3. **Q.** *How do we bring team members up to our level of knowledge and understanding when decisions need to be made yesterday?*

A. You can't and you won't. Team building is a process that requires tremendous patience. We encourage management to explain things over and over, using different examples, visuals, videos—whatever it takes. It's particularly hard not to show frustration or intolerance through one's voice and body language. Sometimes it helps to ask the owner or senior executive how long it took him or her to become savvy about the business—and apply the same number of years for development of staff.

The best results are achieved when trust between the team and management is solid and top management has set up contingencies that allow it to step in when absolutely necessary.

4. **Q.** *How will we know when to let go and let others experiment and even fail?*

   A. Every time an owner, a CEO, or a manager assigns a task to a team, he or she must be clear about the level of authority the team will have (see under "Authority Options" earlier in this chapter). "Letting go" is a gradual process. Proper advance planning and honest, ongoing communication are vital to success.

   Managers who historically have micromanaged every last detail suffer through the letting-go process. That's where it's important to have long-term thinking, rather than focus on immediate results. We've seen teams progress beautifully until the manager gets nervous about a mistake and begins to take back control. People see this response as an example of lack of commitment—"See, you never really meant to create teams at all." They do not realize that managers are struggling with as many behavioral changes as they are, and maybe more.

5. **Q.** *What if management doesn't believe in this stuff?*

   A. People are able to sense ambivalence very quickly. Managers and CEOs forget that employees are always watching everything they do and say and making judgment calls about their commitment on the basis of the employees' interpretation of the behavior.

   If management is split about teams, implementing them won't work, plain and simple. Executives would do better just to practice sound traditional maagement, rather than to send mixed messages. Employees are very wary of programs that come and go overnight. One supervisor recently said, "I'll just bide my time and this will blow over—just like customer service and productivity did."

6. **Q.** *How do we get team members to start talking when we've never encouraged open communication before?*

A. We suggest that you explain to team members where you're coming from and what's going to be expected of them (e.g., more talking, asking questions, working together on the business's problems).

In the beginning, it's important to structure ways for people to start talking. For example, you might ask people to write down what they think customers like best about the business and then share their responses in small groups. The groups can then report their results to everyone.

It's critically important to control any body language that might imply that you disagree with what is being said. We've seen people clam up just because a CEO knitted his brow (he actually was suffering from a headache).

7. **Q.** *How long will it take before we see some real results?*

A. This question is asked more than any other. Most experts suggest it takes three to five years before results are apparent. When organizations have invested substantially in staff training and support, we've seen results much sooner (eighteen months to two years).

It's important to remember that you are creating a cultural (or paradigm) change in the organization. The stages in the process include: (1) awareness of teams as a possibility; (2) acquiring the understanding and knowledge of how teams function; (3) learning the actual skills required so you can perform the new behavior; and (4) internalizing the attitude or value so that functioning as a team is automatic and desired.

Many times it may look as if nothing is happening (especially in the early stages) when in fact a lot is going on.

8. **Q.** *What can we do when the amount of change and knowledge needed to succeed feels overwhelming?*

A. We encourage business owners and managers who are implementing teams to network with each other. Sometimes just hearing the struggles of another business gives a person inspiration and confidence. Besides, real-life situations are much more honest than articles in magazines that imply that teams are formed and functioning overnight.

9. **Q.** *Should we do all the facilitating of meetings?*

A. We recommend that the role of the facilitator be rotated among everyone on a team. Although an owner or manager can facilitate the first meeting to show by example how it should be done, he or she must not hold the leadership role for too long.

Some people shy away from the role of facilitator; we've had people tell us they became physically ill the night before they were to facilitate a meeting. One solution is to allow team members to pass on the first one or two rotations of the facilitator role until they feel more comfortable. A buddy system of cofacilitators can work to reduce members' anxiety; experienced facilitators can coach and train new ones. Once people have performed the facilitator role and felt the team's support, two things happen: It's easier to facilitate the next time, and the tendency to criticize other people's performance as facilitators drops dramatically.

10. **Q.** *Why do first-line supervisors have such a hard time with teams?*

A. The traditional role of the supervisor is to tell others what to do and to inspect to see that it is done right. Most supervisors are promoted to their positions because they were the fastest or the best at the job, not because they were able to work well with others.

When teams are formed, the obvious question for the supervisor is, "What do I do now?" One team even tried to fire its supervisor, partly because of all the anger members had bottled up over the years and partly because they couldn't think of a purpose for him. After a year of discussions and negotiating, the team has now defined his role as subject matter expert, liaison to other departments and management, and coordinator of daily activities. The supervisor has had to learn a new set of people skills and decision-making behaviors. Whereas he used to respond with a prompt yes or no, he now has to decide whether the issue should be brought to the team for decision.

Sometimes supervisors just don't make the transition. Early data suggest that about 25 percent of people experience great difficulty functioning in teams; the loss of control, the patience required, even the willingness to share the credit for results are too much for them. We find most leave on their own accord once they realize the organization is not going to backtrack.

11. **Q.** *What is the value of the process observer role?*

A. Most teams are very able to perform task functions (set goals, develop strategies for achieving goals, assign tasks) and often avoid the relationship functions of the team (communicating, building trust, resolving conflicts).

However, if the team has assigned a person the job of surfacing hidden agendas and other "people" problems, that person is able to say, "As process observer, I need to remind the team about our commitment not to interrupt each other" or to address whatever the issue is.

When the role is not assigned, the check on behavior doesn't happen, and typically the team relationship deteriorates. Often when we ask a team that says it's having difficulty if the team has been using its process observers, the answer is no. Without permission from the team, we find people are hesitant to surface problems with relationship issues because to do so suggests conflict.

12. **Q.** *What if we don't like meeting with staff and prefer an introverted leadership style?*

A. A number of CEOs have difficulty really joining in with their people and functioning on a team. They prefer to remain behind closed doors, communicating with a few key people.

This behavior slows the team process because people spend so much time trying to figure out the CEO's commitment level. One solution is to empower vice presidents who are willing to support the process 100 percent and to carry the organization through the team building steps. This procedure is never as effective as if the president participates.

Another idea is to have someone videotape the president, speaking to the organization's goals and the progress being made, on a regular basis. Although the communication is only one-way, we've seen it help to minimize anxiety about leadership commitment.

13. **Q.** *What do we do if our union opposes teams?*

A. Most experts encourage very early involvement of union officials in the design and planning of the team culture.

Many companies find that a union that formally opposes the use of teams often will not object to its members (employees) being part of a team if it is working on a specific problem. We have experienced problems with at least one union refusing to allow employees to be trained in team building skills.

14. **Q.** *Are there stages that a team goes through as it matures?*

A. Experts (Schein, 1985; Hersey and Blanchard, 1988) all agree that there are four stages teams go through: the formation stage, in which members are trying to decide why they are there; the group-building stage, in which the team decides on its direction and control; a third stage, in which everyone starts to work together; and a final stage, in which the team can function efficiently. Teams can take weeks or months to progress through the stages, depending on how critical their task is and how often they can work together.

15. **Q.** *Do teams develop a special language? Is it okay?*

A. It's very common for teams to use "buzzwords" or special phrases that are intelligible only to other team members. Nothing is wrong with this as long as new members are properly oriented to the special language of the team.

Notes

1. C. A. Aubrey and P. K. Felkins, *Teamwork: Involving People in Quality and Productivity Improvement* (White Plains, N.Y.: Quality Resources, 1988).
2. Teamwork: Your Role in Developing the Winning Edge. Supervisory Skills Program (Waterford, Conn.: Bureau of Business Practice, Inc., 1987).
3. R. F. Hicks and D. Bone, *Self-Managing Teams: Creating and Maintaining Self-Managed Work Groups* (Los Altos, Calif.: Crisp Publications, 1990).
4. C. A. Aubrey and P. K. Felkins, op. cit.
5. L. Miller and J. Howard, *Managing Quality Through Teams: A Workbook for Team Leaders and Members* (Atlanta: Miller Consulting Group, 1991).
6. R. F. Hicks and D. Bone, op. cit.

Chapter 2

Let's Meet: Team Meetings

After a team is formed, its first step is to meet. Most employees have little experience with gathering and discussing and deciding issues as a group. A clear meeting structure that is used over and over again will ease members' anxiety and greatly reduce the time spent in meetings. One example of a team meeting structure is shown in Figure 2-1.

Setting the Agenda

An agenda should always be prepared and distributed before each meeting. There are five steps to follow in setting the agenda:

1. Ask team members for agenda ideas. (We have found that a clipboard on the back of a door works well as a way for team members to write down agenda topics from meeting to meeting.)
2. Review actions agreed upon at previous meetings.
3. Prioritize agenda items and put them in logical sequence; assign tentative times allotted for discussion if possible.
4. Send out the agenda in advance of the meeting to all participants.
5. Make extra copies available during the meeting.

Structuring the Meeting

Q&A #2, 11

The meeting should start on time with a review of the agenda, and any necessary changes should be made by team consensus.

Figure 2-1. Sample team meeting format.

I. Meeting Structure

  a. Review agenda
  b. Set time limits for discussion of agenda items
  c. Assign roles/responsibilities (facilitator, process observers, timekeeper, scribe)
  d. Clarify authority and the team's role (if applicable)

II. Define Goal (expected outcome) for Meeting (do not proceed without a common goal)

III. Return to Structure

  a. Decide on procedure to achieve goal including:
    - Whole-team or small-team discussion
    - Brainstorming and multivoting
    - Type of decision making
    - Special boundaries (breaks)

IV. Proceed With Meeting Agenda

V. Closure

  a. Summation
  b. Follow-up: where do we go from here?
  c. Informing those not present

The facilitator must ask the team what the goal of the meeting is in order to help set priorities for agenda items. Once the agenda has been agreed to, it should be followed; new noncritical items that come up should be set aside for another meeting. The facilitator is responsible for ensuring that the meeting progresses efficiently according to the agenda. The timekeeper is responsible for reminding the team of the time limits for discussion of each agenda item.

Q&A #1

When there is no established goal, teams tend to allow discussion to wander in many different directions, losing valuable team time and frustrating results-oriented team members, who either try to get back on track or withdraw altogether. Every meeting must therefore have an identifiable goal.

The facilitator should conduct the meeting in a manner that encourages participation from all team members. In particular, the facilitator may have to ask shy individuals for their opinions on some issues and remind excessive talkers to share the floor. The facilitator should serve as the catalyst and not speak for more than 25 percent of the meeting time.

Responsibility for taking minutes should be rotated among the members. Some facilitators may feel it is easier and faster to prepare the minutes themselves, but this urge should be resisted. Rotating the scribe/recorder position means that no one person is burdened with documenting all the meetings and allows employees who want to learn business writing to do so.

The minutes should identify discussion points, decisions reached, actions committed to, and deadlines set. Team members should receive copies of the minutes.

The facilitator should avoid having the team vote on issues. Instead, consensus decision making should be used to set directions or to give priority to certain problems. Sometimes an informal show of hands may be helpful. It is very important that the team support the decisions that are made and that all individuals have adequate opportunity to influence the entire team before a firm decision is reached. Problems that divide the team and require more time for research or discussion can be assigned to subgroups, who can later report their findings to the entire team. Q&A #8

The meeting agenda and problems discussed should be restricted to items that are controlled by the team and that affect the team's output. Members should be prepared with the information necessary to discuss all agenda items. If the team's problems are caused by other functional areas, the facilitator should quickly pass this information along to managers in those areas.

The meeting should end on time, with the facilitator reviewing the team's action items and decisions and seeking clarification about how the team wants to handle any leftover agenda items.

The following are the critical process points in team meetings:

1. Select a facilitator, process observers, timekeeper, and scribe.

2. Clarify purpose and set goal for the meeting.
3. Define behaviors that will help or hinder the team's progress.
4. Define step-by-step process to handle the subject; set time limits.
5. Discuss the subject.
6. Explore alternatives.
7. Summarize the discussion.
8. Agree, by consensus, on action to be taken.
9. Identify and assign tasks and/or next steps.

Q&A #9

Handling Leftover Agenda Items

Especially in the beginning, teams often have more items on their agendas than they can handle in a single meeting. To prevent this from being a frustrating and demoralizing problem, the team may choose to use one of the following strategies:

- Assign each member a leftover agenda item, and ask each person to collect materials and prepare handouts before the next meeting.
- Identify the first step to be taken on an item, and assign an owner and a deadline.
- Have each person complete written comments on the agenda item and copy and distribute them to all members before the next meeting. Have the facilitator organize ideas.
- Keep a running flip-chart list of "other agenda items" to avoid losing track of any.
- Limit the agenda to one or two topics, and break down those topics into smaller agenda items.

Special Meeting Tips

Here are some general pointers to keep in mind when you facilitate team meetings:

- Put problems first, planning second, and information sharing last on your agenda.

- Change the agenda only when the entire team agrees, not when only one person suggests a revision.
- If some members do not want to deal with an item, remind the team that it lacks consensus to put it on the agenda.
- If an agenda is amended, insist on a response to the change from the team.
- Be suspicious of agreements reached too easily.
- Hold people to speaking for themselves only (e.g., discourage generalizations like "Some people say . . ." and "We all know . . .").
- In tense situations or when solutions are difficult to reach, remember the value of small-team discussion, humor, quick games for energy, affirmation, and silence.
- End the meeting with a sense of gathering together and a summary.

Handling Specific Issues

Absences

Irregular attendance at meetings by team members is very destructive to the team process. The team's efforts and energies are diverted from working on the goals to figuring out how to move forward when members aren't present. Poor attendance early in the formation of the team is an indicator of problems that may result in the resignation of a member.

Absences occur most often when there is questionable commitment from top management for the team process. We have seen dramatic improvements when team members express their feelings of anger and frustration to late or absent members. Q&A #10

A team member who must miss a meeting or arrive late should, if possible, phone another team member or the meeting site to spare the team from wasting considerable time.

If a member arrives late, the facilitator should stop the meeting and ask a member to update the late arrival on what has happened or been decided so far. When this doesn't occur, the member is left in the dark and cannot be an effective contributor. This is a small and subtle courtesy that helps to shape the team's process of caring and supporting one another. However, having many members arrive late can be disruptive to those team members who arrived on time and may require team discussion.

When a team member has missed a meeting, he or she is required to review minutes and obtain a verbal update from another team member. It is often helpful to assign a team member the task of collecting handouts for and updating the absent member. Some teams establish permanent partners or buddies who keep each other informed and collect handouts and other materials for their absent partner.

Q&A #12

Confidentiality

One of the early decisions a team must make concerns the level of confidentiality it wants to maintain. The following guidelines have proved effective:

In Team Meetings

- Topics are designated confidential when discussion of the topic is completed.
- Members will honor any individual's request for confidentiality.

Outside Team Meetings

- Members may share general information about what was discussed but may not make specific references to what any individual said.
- Members will not share specifics about individuals or individual statements.
- Issues and discussions of the team must be reported to the company, except when designated confidential.
- Video- or audiotapes of meetings may not be shared outside the team unless permission is granted by the team.
- The team will review these rules whenever they become a problem.
- A breach of confidentiality is a serious offense and will result in team disciplinary action.

Maintenance Tasks

On projects or tasks requiring tedious chores, such as stapling or collating, the team should make a rotation schedule so everyone does his or her fair share.

In one group, after a month of being expected to supply coffee for weekly team meetings, two women members surfaced their growing anger and resentment with team members. Although it was difficult for the women to talk about their feelings, the team responded well and decided to rotate all the tasks.

Teams need to guard against putting women members into traditional roles: scribe, gofer, cook, and bottle washer.

Duration and Frequency of Meetings

Q&A #9, 13

The suggested meeting length is no more than two hours. The facilitator and/or process observers should check with the team regarding needed breaks. Frequency of meetings and meeting length vary with team goal, deadline, and individual schedules. The best schedule is usually a weekly meeting lasting no more than one hour.

Meeting Options

Q&A #7, 14

- Brief meetings at the beginning of shifts for between fifteen and thirty minutes
- Two three-hour meetings once or twice a month to discuss specific team issues
- Weekly meetings, lasting from twenty to sixty minutes, to share information and work on improvements and problem solving

Guests

Guests are welcome at meetings with prior notification to any team member. The team member shall notify all members of the team and the facilitator for that particular meeting. Guests should be introduced, presented with a brief summary of the team's tasks, and briefed on confidentiality rules at the start of the meeting by the facilitator.

Leaderless Meetings

If the leader is absent, the team should decide whether to designate a new leader at the start of the meeting or to reschedule the meeting.

Early Departure From the Meeting

The team should discourage members from coming and going at will during a meeting. If late arrival or early departure is necessary, the facilitator should be informed at the start of the meeting.

Openness of Sessions

The team should decide whether its meetings are to be open to outsiders.

Individual Participation

Participation in discussion at team meetings is a requirement for all team members, although the team must be patient in the beginning with individuals who are shy or have difficulty speaking in groups.

If a member has not participated in discussions by the fifth or sixth meeting, the facilitator and process observers may meet with the individual to determine if something is wrong.

Q&A #3, 4

Participation may be encouraged by using any of the following techniques:

1. Rotating all team roles
2. Sitting in a circle or horseshoe design
3. Giving members a limited number of an item (paper clips, toothpicks) and requiring "payment" when the person speaks, thereby restricting members' ability to dominate the group
4. Passing a baton from person to person
5. Brainstorming ideas

6. Going person by person around the room soliciting input
7. Having small-group discussion prior to all-group discussion
8. Asking open-ended questions
9. Calling on people directly
10. Giving out tasks between meeting assignments
11. Using icebreakers

Pay

On occasion, hourly (nonexempt) employees may question whether they will be paid for time spent at team meetings or team training outside the regular workday. In all cases, nonexempt employees participating on teams should be paid their regular wages for time spent on team activities, including overtime pay when appropriate.

Physical Setting

Q&A #16

Team meetings may be held in any setting, provided the room affords privacy and freedom from distraction. Any team member is encouraged to suggest alternative meeting sites. Teams tend to lay claim to fixed sites and familiar places.

The facilitator is typically responsible for reserving space and bringing supplies. Most teams find an easel, flip chart, markers, and masking tape essential to their work.

Poor physical surroundings deter team effectiveness. Traditional classroom seating and standing in an informal group are two formats that don't work. In addition, poor lighting and ventilation, noisy distractions, and a lack of writing space (flip chart, blackboard) can all affect team productivity.

Face-to-face seating is most useful in problem solving. Seating should be designed to increase participation—for example, circle, square, or horseshoe (see Figure 2-2). No one position should be dominant. Team members should feel that they are in a "huddle." Rooms should have walls on which flip-chart paper and graphs can be taped or pinned.

Figure 2-2. Sample seating formats for meetings.

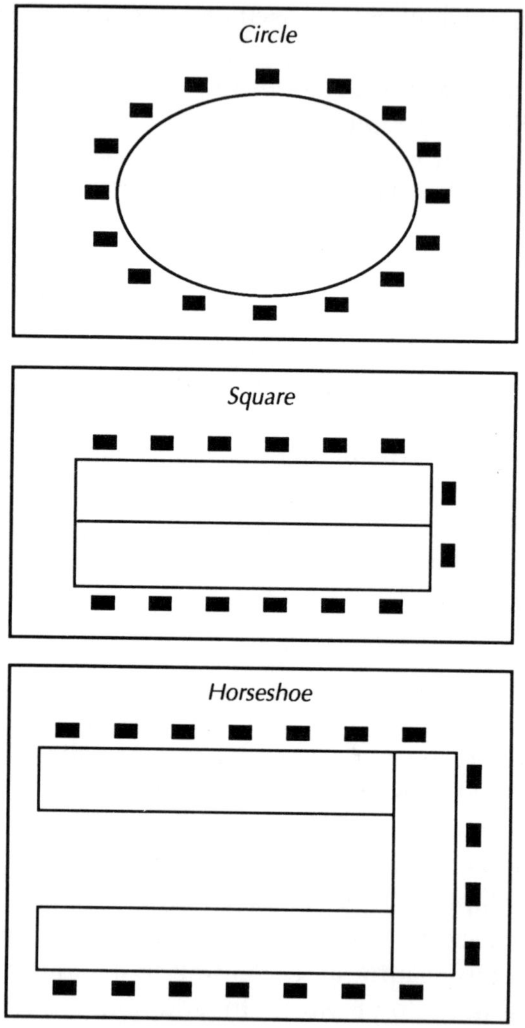

Q&A #5

Subgrouping

Subgrouping (team members meeting informally without the rest of the team) may indicate a considerable degree of hostility in the team, especially toward the leader. For this reason, subgrouping (except on a short-term basis) is to be discouraged.

The only legitimate reason for subgrouping is the need for a small group within the team to complete a specific task assigned by the entire team.

Tardiness

Tardiness is not permitted without prior notice to the facilitator. Tardiness, like irregular attendance, usually signifies resistance. When several members are often late or absent, the team may want to search for the source of the team resistance.

Tardiness is perhaps the most common problem teams have to confront during their first month or two. Team members may need to be reminded that they demonstrate their commitment to the team, in part, by arriving on time, prepared to participate. Chronic tardiness may be a passive/aggressive response to a deeper problem with control. Although it may appear as if the person is showing a lack of respect for the process or for team members, more likely it is a deeper conflict within the individual.

Team Files

Team files may contain minutes, memos, reports, proposals, and works in progress. Rules regarding confidentiality and access to team files should be determined by each team at the start of its work.

Symptoms of Internal Meeting Problems

There are several clues that can tell you something is not right in your team meeting structure and procedures. Among them are these warning signs:

- Team meetings start later and later each time.
- No meeting goal is established in the beginning.
- No agenda exists, or the agenda is not distributed in advance.
- The facilitator is not prepared or monopolizes the discussion.

- Only a few members speak; others withdraw nonverbally.
- The meeting focuses on informational "show and tell," rather than on planning or problem solving.
- Members interrupt each other or "cross-talk," excluding others.
- Additional discussion occurs after the meeting in small group "triangles."
- No conclusions are reached by the team.
- No plan for follow-through is developed.
- No ownership is assigned for agreed-upon tasks.
- Assignments are not completed on time.

Facilitating Meetings

The role of facilitator is critical to the success of a meeting. A skilled facilitator has the ability to ask just the right question to open discussion and keep the team moving. It is critical for the balance of power that the role of facilitator be rotated among team members. (Facilitator behavior is discussed more fully in Chapter 3.)

The following examples provide the facilitator with some useful tools for generating discussion.[1]

1. *Get the meeting started.* "Let's review the agenda, get team assignments, and add or delete any items we need to." "I suggest that we deal with the short items first and then do the project item after a short break. Is that all right?" "Our goal for the meeting today is. . . . Does anyone see it differently?"

2. *Encourage communication and involvement of all members.* "Let's go around the room and get everyone's opinion about. . . ." "How do you feel about this?" "How would you answer that question?" "We haven't heard from you yet. How do you feel about this?"

3. *Ask team members for opinions and feelings to encourage discussion.* "Do you agree with. . . ?" "What is your reaction to. . . ?" "How do you feel about. . . ?" "Would you say that. . . ?" "We've

heard from you already on this topic. Sherri hasn't spoken yet and may want to add something."

4. *Ask for a summary of the discussion.* "A lot of good ideas have been presented in the last half hour. Will someone summarize the major points before we go on?" "I have heard a number of suggestions. Will someone summarize what has been agreed to?" "I think we have gotten off course. Will someone summarize what has been said so far?"

5. *Paraphrase what someone has said to help members understand each other.* "I'm not sure I understand. Are you saying that. . . ?" "What I'm hearing is. . . . Is that right?" "It sounds as if you're asking me to. . . ."

6. *Ask for specific examples to improve understanding.* "Will you give some examples of what you mean?" "Can you expand on that? I'm not sure I understand."

7. *Clarify assumptions.* "Your idea assumes that she will participate." "Your proposal assumes that unless we use threats, they won't cooperate. Is that right?" "Your suggestion assumes that we cannot meet the deadline. Is that right?"

8. *Ask for explanation in order to eliminate confusion and repetition.* "We have been everywhere with this issue. Can someone suggest how we might proceed?" "I didn't understand what you were saying. What would you do if. . . ?" "The examples you gave apply to. . . . Do they also apply to. . . ?" "It's still not clear to me. What do I do when. . . ?"

9. *Probe an idea in greater depth.* "How about a totally different opinion?" "What are some other ways to approach this problem?" "Are there other things we should consider?" "What would you add to what has already been said?"

10. *Suggest a break or rest.* "We have been working on this problem for about an hour. I suggest we take a ten-minute break."

11. *Move the team toward action.* "What would you do first?" "How would you suggest that we proceed on this?" "I'd like some suggestions on possible ways to get started." "How would you propose we get started?"

12. *Poll members.* "How does everybody feel about this?" "How many believe this is an idea worth pursuing?" "Let's ask everyone how they feel about the proposal."

13. *Encourage open-mindedness.* "I don't think you heard what he was trying to say. It might help if you tell us what you heard him say before you state your objections." "Let's go around the table so everyone gets a chance to comment on this."

14. *Recommend a process.* "I suggest we go around the table to see how everyone feels about this issue." "Would it help if we put the agenda items in priority order before we start?" "Let's try brainstorming to get some new ideas on the table."

15. *Step out of the facilitator role.* "I'd like to make a comment—would someone serve as facilitator for a few minutes so I can state my opinion?" "I have strong feelings about this topic and would like to have someone else facilitate."

16. *Stop discussion to focus on team feelings.* "Let's take a break from the tasks for a few minutes and have each of us talk about what he or she is feeling right now." "I'm frustrated. I think we should take this problem up next week when we have more facts. How do the rest of you feel?"

17. *Encourage greater participation.* "Let's give him a chance to tell it the way he sees it." "I believe you've had a chance to speak on this topic already. Some others need a turn."

18. *Reflect for the team what someone else is feeling.* "I get the impression that you are not satisfied with my answer. Is that right?" "Her comments tell me that she needs to ask some questions on this. Is that right?" "It sounds to me as if. . . ."

19. *Get back on track.* "I think we've lost our focus." "How does what we're talking about relate to our agenda item?" "I need help finding a common thread here."

20. *Surface differences of opinion.* "You haven't said so, but it's clear to me that you don't agree. Is that right?" "I'm afraid people are saying what they think others want to hear. What do you think about this?" "You seem to be holding back on this. Is there something here you disagree with?" "I think we're trying to avoid disagreeing with each other. Who would be willing to voice a different opinion?"

21. *Check team progress.* "Are we asking the right question?" "Are these the most important goals?" "Is this the best way to get your support?"

22. *Encourage new thinking.* "Why don't you take the role of a customer for a few minutes? Now, as a customer, how would you react to this proposal?" "Pretend you are the department head for a moment. How would you react to this proposal?" "How would you feel if you were treated this way?"

23. *Explore potential results.* "If we did it this way, what is the worst thing that could happen?" "If it doesn't work, what have we lost?" "If it works, how will it effect our goal?"

24. *Test for consensus of the team.* "Can we identify any areas we still disagree on?" "It seems that we have come to agreement on this issue. Does everyone accept the idea that. . . ?" "Do we have consensus that the best approach is. . . ?" "I sense that we are in agreement. Does anyone see it differently?" "Is this something we can all live with?"

25. *Handle consensus blockers.* "We would like to hear your reasons for blocking the decision. Would you please explain?" "Is there a compromise you would like to offer?" "Would you be willing to stand aside if we did this for a trial period?"

26. *Move toward decision.* "We have considered every possibility; now we must choose from these three alternatives." "We have discussed both sides carefully. It's time we made a choice."

Questions and Answers: Meetings, Making Rules, and Working Together

1. **Q.** *Are there common mistakes made by teams when they hold their meetings?*

   A. Yes, a number of common problems emerge. It's very difficult to get team members to stop and discuss how they want to proceed with a particular item. We call such a plan team structure or process. Many teams jump right in and start talking about a problem or issue and then about midway through the discussion find themselves lost. That's why we stress mapping out the game plan as the first agenda item. We also often have to remind facilitators to revisit the structure throughout the meeting to gain team consensus on how to proceed.

Many teams start meeting without clear goals—either for the team as a whole or for a particular meeting. The lack of a common goal causes more problems with teams than most people realize. Every meeting should have agreed-upon goals.

A third common problem is a team of both management and hourly workers that is facilitated only by management. We suggest that each team member write his or her job title on an index card for collection at the beginning of each meeting so members are reminded that all team members are equal.

A fourth problem is failing to ask the team for its opinion on every issue. Sometimes we assume that a team wants to proceed in a particular way or give priority to a certain agenda item, rather than seeking the approval of all team members.

2. **Q.** *Is there a most effective agenda format?*

A. Too many teams give information sharing, rather than problem solving and planning, the highest priority on the agenda. Information can be shared with team members in countless ways (memos, bulletin boards, notices, flyers, word of mouth). Valuable meeting time should be spent tapping into the collective genius of all the minds present to solve problems and to plan.

3. **Q.** *Do you suggest icebreakers or warm-ups before team meetings?*

A. Icebreakers are terrific, especially with a large team that meets irregularly. They help to break down social barriers and show members the things they have in common with each other. Icebreakers can also be training tools to teach open-mindedness, listening skills, and trust-building behaviors.

4. **Q.** *Can you give some examples of icebreakers?*

A. Here are some that we've found particularly effective:[2]

• *Position in the Family*. Divide the team by those who were first-born, middle child, and baby or only child, and ask them to discuss what they liked best and least about their position in the family.

• *Snag Tag*. Have team members walk about the room with one hand on their hip and the other free at their side. At the cue of the facilitator, members "snag" the elbow of a partner until groups of four or five are formed. Members then sit with their new snag partners. Ideal for breaking up established cliques.

• *Getting to Know You*. Pair up with a partner, and describe two physical attributes you like about yourself, two personality qualities you like about yourself, and one talent or skill you like about yourself. Then have your partner talk about himself or herself.

• *Scavenger Hunt*. Make up a list of ten questions about little-known facts (e.g., How long is the standard cigarette? How many red stripes on the American flag?), and then work in small groups for ten minutes to find the answers.

• *Bingo Card*. Write something about each member on a bingo-style card. Members have to find the person who signs the card in the square about themselves. The winner is the person who gets squares signed in a diagonal, vertical, or horizontal row.

• *Circle Within a Circle*. Each person develops a list of incomplete statements (e.g., the thing I like best about this team is . . .). The team is then divided into two concentric circles that face each other. Team members greet each other nonverbally, the facilitator reads the statement, the person on the outside circle answers the statement, the partners close nonverbally, and the outside circle moves one person counterclockwise. The process then debriefs by having members talk about such things as how they felt or what was the easiest or hardest statement to answer.

5. **Q.** *Should a team stay in a large group to discuss issues, or should it divide into small groups?*

   A. We have found that most teams like to stay together even when they are large so that they can hear everything that is said. It's important that the team experiment and decide how to proceed.

   It can be effective to use subgroups when a team lacks meeting time to develop and/or research an idea. A representative small subgroup can work between scheduled meetings and bring drafts and proposals back to the entire team for consideration.

   Subgrouping is frowned upon when the team is experiencing personality conflicts and subgroups are formed only to vent individual frustrations and divide members into cliques.

6. **Q.** *What if a person won't relinquish the facilitator's role?*

   A. The team will have to surface this problem, either by having the team's process observers meet individually with the team member or by talking about it as a whole team.

   Many managers and first-line supervisors have difficulty letting go of the facilitator or leadership role. Some contend that no one else knows how to handle the role. We recommend that one or two team members talk privately with the individual first and make it a team issue only if the person remains uncooperative.

7. **Q.** *Is it good for a team to meet every morning for a few minutes?*

   A. Yes, communication is a cornerstone of effective teamwork. We know of an organization that has five-minute "toolbox" meetings every morning for its self-directed work teams to set daily goals and surface any pressing problems. For multi- and cross-functional teams it is unrealistic to plan to meet every day.

8. **Q.** *Why is voting such a big no-no?*

   A. When we vote, there is a winner and a loser. In addition to the fact that losers usually like to get even, a team with winners and losers is a divided team with two different goals—doomed for failure.

We do say that teams can have straw polls on occasion to get a general sense of a team's opinion, particularly in the early stages of discussion.

9. **Q.** *What if we underestimate the amount of time something is going to take on the agenda?*

   A. That happens more often than not. In a traditional organization, the meeting chairperson decides to either call it to a vote or move on to the next item. In a team structure, the timekeeper reminds the facilitator of how much time remains for discussion. The facilitator suggests to the team that the time remaining is not sufficient to end discussion on the item and asks the team how it wishes to proceed. The team may choose either to continue discussion by apportioning time from another agenda item or to table the item and put it on the next meeting's agenda.

10. **Q.** *What should you do when members have conflicts with the meeting schedule?*

    A. No team will always be able to have everyone present for all meetings. However, it is important to make sure members who have a strong interest in a particular topic or issue are able to attend a team meeting when it is on the agenda. For example, one team member was angry with his team because it had forgotten to give him particular information. When the team scheduled the next meeting, he said he had a conflict and wouldn't be able to attend. The team decided to go ahead anyway. We reminded the team of member's earlier feelings and asked it to consider how he might be feeling now. It immediately decided to meet when he was available.

11. **Q.** *Does the team always have to agree on the agenda?*

    A. Yes, otherwise the meeting belongs to someone else.

12. **Q.** *What if a team keeps something confidential from management?*

A. That's why it's so important to get the rules straight up front. Management needs to define the boundaries it expects a team to observe.

We encourage teams to be open about the topics of discussion and the issues addressed, while leaving out specific names of who said what to whom.

13. **Q.** *We have so many meetings there is no time to do regular work. What can we do?*

A. A number of ideas come to mind: Discuss as a team the possibility of rotating membership or using substitutes; decide how much time any employee should be spending in meetings and encourage employees not on teams to join new ones; assess the team's time management effectiveness during meetings and develop improved systems to save valuable minutes.

14. **Q.** *What are the different types of meeting options, and when is each most effective?*

A. There are several options:

- *Early morning "toolbox" meetings.* Team meets for five to ten minutes to set priorities and surface any problems.
- *Weekly team meetings.* Team meets for about an hour working from a prepared agenda. Team examines week's results and discusses some advance planning.
- *Biweekly or monthly quality meetings.* Team spends time on one or two critical quality problems and develops strategies for improvements.

15. **Q.** *Some meetings are a lot tougher than others because of tension on the team or whatever. Are there special tips for handling tough meetings?*

A. Choose an experienced facilitator who can handle difficult people well. The facilitator should structure the session tightly, beginning with a complete buy-in on the goal (expected outcomes) for the session. Then ask for suggestions about procedures and special boundaries. Be sure to use the process observers and have help/hinder sheets on the table. The facilitator should review his or her role, including any ground rules needed before proceeding.

16. **Q.** *Are there special seating patterns that work well for teams?*

A. Research says that teams should sit in circles, ovals, horseshoes, or any other format that encourages discussion and equality.

17. **Q.** *Is it ever worthwhile to have an outsider critique a team meeting?*

A. Absolutely. An outsider can often identify specific interpersonal dynamics that are holding back a team. It's important that an outsider be assertive enough to point out behavioral and structural problems and be able to handle any defensiveness from team members. All criticism should be very specific in description and should suggest a better way of handling a similar situation next time.

Sample Questions

"What areas of the team's effort caused particular difficulty and why?"
"What areas of the team's effort were handled particularly well and why?"
"What can the team do next time to improve results?"

18. **Q.** *Can a team assess its own ability?*

A. There are a number of excellent self-assessment tools for teams. The "Team Effectiveness Profile" (TEP)[3] put out by Organization Design and Development, Inc., is particularly effective for diagnosing how members feel the team is progressing in five key areas:

1. Group mission, planning, and goal setting
2. Group organization
3. Group operating processes
4. Group interpersonal relationships
5. Intergroup relations

Assessment tools are a helpful way to get discussion started when problems exist in team relationships. The tool becomes a benign entity that helps members avoid personal attacks. It also helps convince members who would prefer to deny that problems and conflicts exist.

19. **Q.** *What role should owners or managers play in a team meeting?*

A. We encourage the team to discuss the issue right up front and decide as a team what the specific role should be. For example, we've had teams describe the owner's role as involving listening, responding, clarifying expectations and disappointments, defining the big picture and long-range plan, demonstrating open-mindedness, and being active but not overpowering.

Similarly, managers need to discuss and even negotiate their roles with specific teams. All of this is new to both sides, so it is wise to anticipate some uncomfortableness and anxiety.

Once we saw a team develop a long "to do" list describing the manager's role. He was the person who they thought should organize everything, resolve all the conflicts, interact with other teams, and so on. When it came time to negotiate, he was wise enough to say "no" to more than half the items on the list, explaining why it was important for other members to share the responsibility. The appearance of the team visibly changed as he empowered them with new authority.

Notes

1. M.E. Haynes, *Effective Meeting Skills. A Practical Guide for More Productive Meetings* (Los Altos, Calif.: Crisp, 1988).
2. C. R. Mill, *Activities for Trainers, 50 Useful Designs* (San Diego, Calif.: University Associates, 1980); J. W. Newstorm and E. E. Scannell, *Games Trainers Play* (New York: McGraw-Hill, 1980).
3. R. Glaser and C. Glaser, "Team Effectiveness Profile," 2d ed. (King of Prussia, Pa.: Organization Design and Development, Inc., 1980, 1984).

Chapter 3
Team Behavior

Americans do not grow up learning how to function in teams. In school we never receive a team report card or learn the names of the team of sailors who traveled with Columbus to America. As the author Marvin Weisbord said, "Teamwork is the quintessential contradiction of a society grounded in individual achievement."[1]

Teamwork places tremendous demands on interpersonal skills. It requires open, honest, direct communication; the ability to surface issues and to resolve conflicts; and an understanding of one's own and others' feelings.

It's not uncommon for about 20 or 30 percent of the employees involved on teams to struggle and resist the demands that they change their behaviors.[2] Some eventually grow dramatically and achieve tremendous results; others end up finding jobs in more traditional environments. Q&A #1, 3

Very early in the team process, members must define what will be acceptable behavior and what won't. Inattention to the relationship functions in the team is a primary cause of problems later on and often prevents a team from maturing properly.

Team Rules of Behavior

Q&A #2

Each team begins by developing its own code of conduct or help/hinder list—a set of acceptable and unacceptable behaviors (see Figure 1-2). The code is designed to:

- Create common expectations and understanding among members
- Encourage desirable behavior
- Enhance the self-management of the team
- Provide a written record of guidelines
- Help new members know what's expected
- Bring problem behavior back into line

Q&A #7

The process observers are the guardians of the help/hinder list and can at any time surface counterproductive behaviors simply by waving the list during a meeting. In the early stages of team building, the help/hinder list should be reviewed regularly (every eight weeks) and discussed by the team.

Many team members who are new to the team process snicker when they start to write a help/hinder list. They suggest, somewhat arrogantly, that everyone knows how to behave. Then a shy member will bravely say, "No, we don't." The silence is deafening, and then everyone gets busy on the list.

An essential element of team behavior is that all team members are encouraged to express themselves in an open, honest, and direct manner, recognizing the interdependence of all team members.

Acceptable Team Behavior

- Making "I" statements such as "I feel," "I think," "I need"
- Active listening to promote two-way communication
- Respecting others' needs, feelings, and rights by allowing others to disagree
- Sharing information and expertise openly

On the other hand, team members cause great difficulty when they exhibit behaviors that are not conducive to the efforts of the team as a whole. Some typical examples follow.

Unacceptable Team Behavior

- Unwilling to set aside personal needs or agendas and work with the rest of the team

- Aggressively using "always" or "never" to intimidate other members
- Displaying a negative attitude toward change, people, and team building in general
- Showing a need or strong preference to be the star rather than to be a part of the process
- Judging others quickly, while being slow to examine his or her own behavior

Team building requires that we change our assumptions about people. Often traditional organizations establish rules that suggest employees will be dishonest, steal, show disrespect, cheat, and satisfy only their own needs. In a team building culture, people must be viewed as honest, straightforward, kind, and eager to do the right thing. In the beginning, people will need to challenge their own assumptions in order to change behavior.

Behavior Changes

Teamwork becomes particularly difficult when members recognize that they will each have to change some parts of their behavior. The strongest resistance will occur as the day for changing draws closer. Making excuses, procrastinating, blaming, and feigning ignorance are just a few of the stall tactics members will use. Q&A #4

Critical Behavior Changes for Employees

- Learning to speak up in groups
- Taking responsibility for own thoughts/actions
- Learning to state an opinion
- Receiving and expressing positive and negative feelings
- Saying no
- Responding to criticism
- Making requests of authorities
- Negotiating for something desired

Critical Behavior Changes for Supervisors

- Being willing to share power and responsibility
- Proposing ideas for discussion
- Asking questions
- Listening to others
- Remaining open-minded

Q&A #5, 9

Critical Behavior Changes for Managers

- Having the courage to resist recommendations that are not beneficial
- Accepting decentralized decision making
- Believing that everyone has good ideas
- Being willing to implement team suggestions whenever possible
- Recognizing team accomplishments
- Seeing teams as a long-term effort

There is a push-pull phenomenon that exists as people experiment with new behavior. As much as we might desire a change in behavior from someone else (the push), we resist it (the pull) because the dynamics of the relationship will also have to change if the behavior of a participant changes. For example, if an autocratic, demanding boss gradually learns to be participatory and inclusive, the team member will have to change all their previous assumptions and conclusions about the boss. For whatever reason, most people will hold back, waiting for the manager to revert to old behavior, and may even try to lure the manager back to old behavior just to be able to say, "I told you so!"

Q&A #6

Team Member Rights

Sometimes it is helpful for the team to develop a list of team member rights. The rights can be posted in order to reinforce desired behavior. Typical rights are these:

- We have the right to support members emotionally while disagreeing with them intellectually.
- We have the right to criticize ideas, but not people.

- We have the right to say what we think, whether others agree or not.
- Conflicts will occur. We have the right to try to learn and grow from them.
- We have the right to expect others to try to overcome avoidance and to deal with conflicts.
- We have the right to expect members to try to participate and to work to become more involved.
- We have the right to expect we are all equal members; no one member's ideas are any greater than another's, and all will be subject to the same scrutiny.
- We have the right to expect that people will leave their "power" (e.g., position and title) outside the team.
- We have the right to express our feelings without being told we "should" feel a different way.
- We have the right to expect that the process will take a long time and that periodically we will make mistakes.

Team Member Expectations

Team members often develop unrealistic expectations about the team process. Expectations should be surfaced, discussed, and evaluated on a regular basis to avoid disappointment.

Realistic Expectations

- Team members will pitch in and help if asked.
- This process, once started, will never end.
- Everyone in the organization will be affected by the change to a team culture.
- Things are worse than they've ever been (in the team's early stages).
- Everyone is stressed out and uptight.
- We'll never go back to the old way.

Unrealistic Expectations

- Team members will pitch in and help out without being asked.
- Everything will be great.

- We'll all support each other on every issue.
- Nobody will ever get fired again.
- Somebody will bring coffee without being asked.

Sometimes the level of misapprehension can be surprising. For example, a company discharged a poorly performing team member and did not anticipate the staff reaction. Apparently, team members had assumed that no one would get fired in a team environment. Although no one could identify where the assumption had originated, it took considerable discussion and explanation to diffuse the anger.

Team Member Behavior

Team members are not expected to exhibit perfect team behavior in the beginning. Rather, team members need to show a willingness to explore new approaches.

Helpful Member Behaviors

- Willingness to participate, contribute ideas, and set goals
- Willingness to rely on and learn to trust other team members
- Willingness to communicate effectively
- Willingness to share and value different ideas
- Willingness to consider other viewpoints
- Willingness to delay judgment
- Willingness to tolerate confusion
- Willingness to seek alternatives that all can agree to
- Willingness to support and implement the team's decisions

Q&A #6

When providing feedback to others about the impact of their behavior on the team, team members should:

- Describe, rather than judge
- Be specific, rather than general
- Be aware of the importance of timing

- Take into account both their needs and those of their listeners
- Suggest a remedy or new behavior
- Check to ensure their communication is clearly understood
- Check to determine whether others agree with you

There are a number of behaviors that are considered counterproductive to any team effort and that should not be tolerated.

Destructive Member Behaviors

1. *Attacking personality.* Redirect the member's focus to a performance issue or problem and away from personal attributes.
2. *Agreeing with everything.* Ask the member to play devil's advocate and express the opposite point of view.
3. *Being inconsistent.* Seek to clarify all apparent inconsistencies by simply stating, "I'm confused."
4. *Binding others' behavior.* Remind a member who says, "You're going to love this idea" to speak for himself or herself; consider trying to surface the "bind."
5. *Changing the subject without explanation.* Point out the need to return to the agenda; suggest putting new topic on the agenda for a later time.
6. *Chatting.* Stop noncontributive talking by team members. Facilitator could ask, "Did you have something you wanted to contribute?"
7. *Complaining.* Ask the person to express his or her concerns; say that negativity is hindering whole team and ask, "Do you have an idea?" Give response and support.
8. *Criticizing.* Take the criticism to the team meeting, and discuss whether it is warranted. If it is, make changes in the way the job is done. If not, remind the member that criticism hinders team progress.
9. *Displaying anger.* Stop the process, acknowledge the anger, and ask its source.
10. *Displaying superiority/dominating.* Recognize the value of the member's input, and move process toward involving the rest of the team.

11. *Engaging in distractions* (doodling, writing memos, doing other work, and making other displays of lack of interest). Ask team member for input in order to bring him or her back into the process.
12. *Escaping* (taking calls, etc.). Ask the member if there is a better time to meet when he or she could give the team full attention.
13. *Explaining the speaker's behavior.* The speaker may state, "I'll explain my own behavior," or another member may remind the team member to speak only to his/her own behavior or opinions.
14. *Frequent head shaking.* Anyone can identify the member and ask why he or she is disagreeing.
15. *Glossing over problems.* Encourage team to explore difficulties and their causes.
16. *Goofing off.* Redirect member's attention back to the process.
17. *Hairsplitting.* Acknowledge that a consensus has been reached, and move process forward.
18. *Interrupting.* State ground rules, and reinforce members' speaking one at a time.
19. *Making decisions without the team's knowledge.* State disapproval of that method; remind member(s) about importance of team involvement in decision-making process.
20. *Misinterpreting* (misstatement of ideas or suggestions by process observers or facilitator). Be assertive about own viewpoint.
21. *Missing many meetings.* Process observers or facilitator can ask why; see if there is a problem (too busy or loss of interest). Reinforce team concept; point out assets of having the person there; point out some of the positives done for the team.
22. *Not completing tasks on time.* Ask if other team members can help; give member a second chance to do the task or allow him or her to back out; talk about accountability.
23. *Not doing a job in a responsible way.* Talk to the member and clarify expectations; set quality standards for how the job is to be done by everyone, every time.

24. *Not participating in team decisions.* Process observers or facilitator talk to member and ask if there is a problem and seek member's involvement in decision-making process.
25. *Not taking the process seriously.* State that each member is expected to value the process enough to spend time discussing the issues.
26. *Offering putdowns.* Explore why the person has that point of view; ask the person to contribute information and options, rather than judgment.
27. *Prejudging.* Note that conclusion is being reached before data are in; acknowledge feelings; seek person's involvement and input.
28. *Pretending not to understand in order to avoid being part of the decision.* Ask member what he or she needs in order to be able to participate in the decision. Do not allow member to abdicate.
29. *Raising false hopes.* Set expectations that are realistic.
30. *Seeking sympathy.* Surface behavior by asking team member what he or she needs from the team.
31. *Seeing only one way ahead.* Ask person to explore other options.
32. *Solving others' problems.* Encourage the person to let others suggest their own solutions.
33. *Speaking in "shoulds."* Redirect focus to what to do next, given the realities.
34. *Suggesting a relationship between subjects when none is apparent.* Ask member to explain how he or she sees the topics relating.
35. *Talking too much.* Ask person to state points one at a time.
36. *Withdrawal.* Ask to hear from members who haven't shared their ideas yet.

One of the classic ways for a team member to resist change or delay a difficult decision is to employ various disruptive behaviors. New teams are particularly vulnerable to this kind of behavior and may need help from experienced teams in managing members' behavior.

Facilitator Behavior

Facilitation skills develop through experience and training. Typically, facilitators find the first couple of meetings difficult. One of the benefits of rotating the facilitator role is that team members tend to be less critical when they know that their own turn will come up quite soon.

Helpful Facilitator Behaviors

1. *Appearing interested.* Assume an alert body position, demonstrating facial expressions and body gestures that convey an active interest in the team and in the progress being made. Openly listen, and pay attention to participants. Be alert to verbal and nonverbal clues in others, such as tone of voice, pauses, gestures, facial expressions, and posture.
2. *Confronting.* Confront inappropriate behavior such as labeling or judgmental statements and responses, especially if an individual's personality is being attacked.
3. *Correcting.* Check inappropriate behavior of group members, and reinforce productive behavior whenever possible.
4. *Evaluating.* Summarize what has happened in the team to this point; evaluate the team's decisions.
5. *Modeling.* Set the behavior standard for the team; demonstrate trust, openness, and cohesiveness, as well as a goal-oriented focus.
6. *Observing team's needs.* Short silences or special activities can be appropriate, giving members time to process information.
7. *Offering support.* Reinforce the statements of others by asking open-ended questions and encouraging the tolerance of new ideas.
8. *Prompting.* Use questions and comments as a way of stimulating discussion and deeper thought.
9. *Refocusing.* Redirect comments to the whole team, especially when a team member's comments are directed at the facilitator.

An untrained or inexperienced facilitator may exhibit many unproductive behaviors. Teams typically have considerable difficulty surfacing these behaviors in a group setting; it is better to have the process observers talk to the facilitator in private. If the facilitator happens to have considerable positional power, it is especially difficult to get team members to discuss the behavior problems openly.

Destructive Facilitator Behaviors

1. *Arguing with team members.* Continued conflicts with a team member; repeatedly turning to one team member for support; ignoring suggestions of certain team members.
2. *Being too easygoing about role.* Being unprepared to facilitate; being late or missing meetings; being uninvolved with the team, as shown by overly relaxed body language and little or no eye contact.
3. *Giving priority to own agenda items.* Interpreting other's comments to support own agenda; continually changing the topic; suggesting similarities between the team discussion and own agenda.
4. *Lacking good team manners.* Not updating a late-arriving team member; taking calls or doing other work while trying to facilitate.
5. *Letting the team wander for long periods.* Providing no direction or help with closure; not defining role up-front; offering pointless comments, humor, or rambling stories; allowing cross-talk between team members.
6. *Manipulating and controlling discussion.* Making statements such as "Some teams are . . ." or "Some teams have . . ."; making suggestions without clearly identifying them as such; making "You should" statements.
7. *Minimizing roles of others.* Neglecting others, including process observers; putting down members; criticizing a member's comments; trying to "one-up" a team member.
8. *Neglecting needs of team members.* Not protecting a team member when he or she is under attack; letting one

member monopolize the discussion; not checking that all members have handouts.

9. *Putting team members into categories.* Dealing with the person rather than the attitude; always calling on the same people to do certain tasks.
10. *Telling the team what to do.* Deciding on the agenda; monopolizing discussion; offering long-winded explanations and making reference to prior teams; imposing specific solutions on the team.
11. *Violating team rules.* Giving a double message of "We're not supposed to but . . ."; selective forgetting of rules.

People typically hesitate to intervene when a facilitator is doing a poor job. However, it is well worth trying to get on track by doing one of the following:

- Have process observers interrupt and state needs of team.
- Call for a break, and have several members talk to facilitator.
- Ask team to evaluate its progress, and provide feedback to all members.
- Have an outside consultant say what team members are not yet able to surface.

Q&A #10, 11

Managing Team Conflict

Most people have considerable difficulty surfacing and working through problems and conflicts. They "collect stamps"—or little injustices—for long periods of time and use passive-aggressive tactics (procrastination, perfectionism, stubbornness, sniping) to surface their difficulty.

In teams, group conflict cannot be shoved under the rug. Process observers must be empowered by the team to surface conflicts and problems while they are still minor in proportion. A simple wave of the help/hinder list has been known to bring behavior back in line.

Conditions Required for Conflict Resolution

- Shared power; sometimes, neutral resource (person/place)
- Recognition of the interdependence of all parties
- Voluntary participation
- Adequate time
- Careful preparation
- Real gains

Key Behavior Agreements Required for Conflict Resolution

- Willingness to listen and to focus on the problem, rather than on the person
- Willingness to define the problem
- Willingness to allow some anger and hostility to surface during discussion
- Willingness to commit to decisions
- Willingness to accept that one might be a part of the problem
- Willingness to try to change behavior

On occasion, members may experience serious difficulty with each other. Personality conflicts or irritable behaviors can undermine the team's efforts unless they are dealt with openly and directly. Here are a few methods for structuring conflict resolution sessions:

Method One. One successful way of surfacing individual behavior conflicts on the team is to ask each person to comment on the following for each member of the team:

- What does Person *X* do that you like particularly?
- What does Person *X* do that creates difficulty for you?
- What could Person *X* do differently?
- What do you count on from Person *X* for the team's success?

Responses to these questions are read and discussed aloud for each member. Each member is encouraged to identify one behavior he or she is willing to work on to improve team effectiveness.

Method Two. If behavior problems continue, we usually encourage the facilitator and the process observers to hold a private meeting with the individual involved and to clearly address the behavior change needed. The discussion should include:

- A report on the person's behavior in specific detail ("Yesterday at our meeting, you openly attacked a team member's idea")
- A statement describing the impact of the behavior on the individual and on the rest of the team ("That type of behavior is not acceptable to the team")
- A specific description of what the person should do ("When you have a strong viewpoint about an idea, we prefer that . . .")
- Identification of the consequences if the person chooses to continue the behavior ("We really believe you can learn different behaviors because we have all had to do the same. If you can't, however, we may have to consider replacing you with another member.")

Method Three. In a team setting, members can surface a problem or conflict by using the following strategy:

- A member surfaces the problem for discussion. Team members define the problem as each sees it, looking for common interpretations.
- Each member speaks to how others on the team contribute to the problem.
- Each member speaks to how he or she contributes to the problem.
- Each member identifies the behavior change needed and makes a commitment to a "first step."
- Follow-up occurs on a regular basis with praise for the effort made.

We have found that young teams need to maintain a strong balance between relationship activities (such as conflict resolution) and task activities. The length of time members can sustain open discussion of conflict varies substantially with the team's prior history and training.

Often teams need a rest from conflict. In the beginning, it is wise to have a trained facilitator handle team conflicts.

Disciplinary Action

Q&A #12, 13

Self-managed teams may occasionally need to discipline team members for misconduct on the job. The team therefore needs an agreed-upon process that encourages it to handle the problem before management becomes involved. Here is a sample ten-step process. Note that throughout the discussion, it is essential for all members to be treated fairly, with consideration and courtesy; issues should be discussed openly and frankly.

1. If a team member has a conflict with another team member, he or she speaks informally with the other person involved within a reasonable period of time. If not satisfied with the results of the discussion, the team member brings the problem to the team facilitator.
2. The team facilitator arranges a meeting of the parties to discuss the problem. No meeting should be held until all parties involved can attend.
3. The facilitator has the option to bring in the team leader/supervisor or another member or to call a team meeting. The facilitator may not evaluate the legitimacy of the problem.
4. A summary of the discussion and any decision(s) reached is written up and given to all involved parties and to the team leader/supervisor; the summary is signed by all. (The summary may be written as a contract to demonstrate the member's commitment to change his or her behavior.)
5. The team member is given a chance to correct the problem.
6. If the member feels wrongly accused, he or she can: (a) go to the facilitator and request a team meeting, (b) go to

the team leader/supervisor, or (c) go to the process observers, who become the advocates.

7. The team leader/supervisor reviews and follows up after fifteen days to see if the behavior has stopped. If so, the person is reunited with the team, and the changed behavior is recognized and praised.
8. If the problem has not stopped, the team signs and sends a written letter expressing its concern and offering two weeks for the person to correct the behavior.
9. If the behavior problem still continues, the situation is referred to the traditional disciplinary policy.
10. If the problem is repeated, the team member goes directly to management for handling.

QUESTIONS AND ANSWERS: Handling a Variety of Behavior Problems

1. **Q.** *Why is team behavior so new for most of us?*

A. The way we behave at work has been greatly influenced by our family backgrounds and our school experiences. Most of us grew up in traditional homes with dad as the strongest authority figure, mom second, and older siblings third. Rules were created by the parents, and we learned to obey them. Occasionally, we might have tried to oppose a rule—only to experience considerable distress.

The same authoritarian structure existed in school. In addition, performance was measured on an individual basis. We can all remember the "smartest kid in class." Report cards were a reflection of individual achievement. By the end of grade school, the "social conduct" skills were no longer measured. The teacher represented authority and the source of correct answers. Few assignments involved working with peers and receiving a team grade for the results.

In school we also learned that there was one right answer and that we could stop looking after we found it. In contrast, teamwork requires us to see several possible answers and to merge ideas in order to achieve consensus.

In team training we conduct an exercise in which we ask people to identify how important speaking, listening, reading, and writing are to their current jobs. Most say that speaking and listening are critically important. We then ask how much formal schooling they have had in these two areas. Typically, most say a few hours or maybe one college course, in marked contrast to the years spent on reading and writing skills. People then begin to see how little skill they have in relation to the work of building teams.

The more people have vested in the traditional paradigm and in the success they have achieved through it, the more resistant they will be toward new behavior requirements.

2. **Q.** *Do rules of conduct really work to control behavior?*

A. Some time ago a team was defining its rules of behavior. One member mentioned how distracting it was when another member doodled during team discussions. The doodler objected, stating that he just liked to draw and that he, indeed, was listening to what people said. Others then mentioned that, while he might be listening, they didn't feel as if he was. Surrounded by pressure from his peers on the team, the doodler chose to comply with the team's request.

We suggest that the help/hinder list developed by each team be copied on colored paper so process observers can easily find and wave the colored list when problems occur. Interestingly, one team that used this method was meeting in a restaurant about a year later when one member started to cross-talk with another. The process observer simply lifted a napkin to signal a problem, and the behavior immediately stopped.

Rules of conduct work well when the team members consistently require members to obey the rules. If the rules of conduct are made but never strongly upheld, the old behaviors will return. It's very difficult for team members to sanction certain behavior because they fear that conflict will result. Most would rather quietly resent the team member for continuing to misbehave. An outside facilitator is often needed to guide the process of getting team members to be more honest with each other.

3. **Q.** *Are there some people who never get it?*

A. Yes, there are some people who refuse to change. In every case they have ended up leaving the organization for a more traditional environment or finding a job within the organization that doesn't require teamwork. The period of time before the individual decides what to do, though, is particularly difficult for the team.

There are others who don't outwardly refuse to change but seem unwilling to work very hard at it. They actually cause more problems because members keep expecting them to get better. "Why does he still do that?" or "Isn't she ever going to learn?" are common refrains. That's when team members need to be reminded that everyone progresses at his or her own pace and that some people are going to take the full three- to five-year time frame to get there.

4. **Q.** *Is there a process that people go through intellectually before the results appear in behavior?*

A. Most experts agree that there are four levels of learning. The first is awareness, when an individual becomes conscious of the fact that a new behavior is desired or required. The individual, at this point, has little or no ability to produce the desired behavior. The team member might say, "Gosh, I don't think they liked what I said."

The second level is understanding and knowledge, when an individual develops the mental understanding and cause-and-effect connections to place the behavior into a particular context. The team member at this level might say, "I think they didn't like the way I said, 'You better do this and you better do that.' "

The third level is skill, when the individual learns how to apply and perform a new behavior. The team member might say, "Rather than using 'you' statements, I think I'll try to say, 'I feel that. . . .' "

The fourth level of learning is attitudes or values, when

the individual wants to perform the new behavior and can make the behavior occur automatically. In this case the member would not use "you" statements at all but would choose "I" statements right from the beginning.

This process goes at different speeds for different people and in different circumstances. Most people get particularly frustrated when they are aware that a new behavior is required but aren't able to do it automatically. Team members who can be supportive and patient with each other will see far greater improvement than those who criticize each other and press for instantaneous improvements.

5. **Q.** *What if a team's behavior is better than management's and the team is saying, "What about those guys?"*

A. This problem occurs more often than the textbooks would like us to believe. Too many managers are not very introspective when it comes to their own behavior. The aggressive and arrogant attitudes that won them rave reviews from their bosses destroy them as team members.

Teams need a particular environment to function well, just like the earth does. For example, poor management behavior is like a pollutant that reduces the speed and level of success. Some organizations tolerate the pollutant and make no effort to neutralize it. Others spend great sums just to contain the problem; others ship the problem promptly to the dump.

The person with the greatest impact by far is the CEO or president. If he or she is an introvert and rarely attends team meetings, this behavior will negatively impact the team. Like it or not, members will spend energy trying to figure out whether the CEO is committed to team building and will adjust the effort spent on changing behavior on the basis of the effort made at the top.

6. **Q.** *What can you do when lapses occur in team behavior?*

A. As teams progress through various stages of maturation, behavior changes. For example, in the early stage team members are ultrapolite with each other, often agreeing with each other just to appear friendly. As the team becomes more focused on specific tasks and the outcome takes on greater importance, members begin to express their differences of opinion, which may be perceived as argumentative and controlling. Only as a team and its members mature in group process do they welcome the give-and-take of discussion and disagreement.

When lapses occur, members of a mature team have the ability to receive feedback, apologize, forgive, and move forward in quick order. However, in an immature team, lapses in behavior are typically talked about outside the team, where members speculate about lack of commitment, unwillingness to work on new behaviors, personality conflicts, and so on, without bringing the problem in an open way to the team. Without meaning to, they are sabotaging the team's future.

It's important for team members to work continually on their interpersonal skills: making "I" statements, developing listening skills, fostering open, honest, and direct communication, finding mutually supported alternatives, and building trust. When lapses occur too regularly, they should serve as a warning sign that the team needs refresher training in team behaviors.

7. **Q.** *What if somebody thinks one of the help/hinder behaviors is ridiculous?*

A. Let's use humor as an example. People have very mixed feelings about humor: Some see it as a way of lightening a mood and keeping everybody happy; others see it as fake and glib. Let's say a team member wants to have humor put on the hinder list. Another member opposes the suggestion, saying that he likes to make jokes and play tricks—fighting the "all work and no play" philosophy.

We encourage the team to talk about the behavior and see how everybody feels. The only objection may be humor that really isn't funny or that has sexual overtone. Sometimes simply redefining or clarifying the problem makes the differences go away. Unity is critically important to successful teams; every effort should be made to talk issues through to a consensus.

8. **Q.** *What if some people have no patience for the "touchy-feely" stuff?*

   A. We had a group of engineers like that several years ago who went through the circle-within-the-circle exercise where they had to complete sentences and share their feelings. At the end, they all decided it was a ridiculous exercise with absolutely no value to the organization; they even questioned our expertise for selecting such a worthless exercise. Well, whenever people are that vocal in their objections, there is usually something underneath they are trying to hide.

   Several months ago the same group contacted us to say that they were having great difficulty with the way team members were relating to each other. The team coordinator wondered if some of the early exercises could be repeated to help team members surface their real feelings. Apparently, there had been a long-standing rivalry between two of the engineers that flared up every time the team needed to make a team presentation.

9. **Q.** *What if one member with considerable power—such as a CEO—is out of control?*

   A. This is an extremely difficult situation for a team, and one with no quick and simple answer.

   Here are some things to try:

   - Make sure the team has a clearly defined goal (specific, measurable, achievable, results-oriented, time-based).
   - Set clear agenda boundaries for every meeting.
   - Select strong facilitators and process observers who will try to redirect some of the behavior.
   - Hold one-on-one sessions with a few influential team members who can have a heart-to-heart with the CEO.
   - Revisit some of the earlier relationship training to remind members of behavior commitments.

- Hold a group session facilitated by an outside skilled facilitator who can help get the issues on the table.
- View a good video such as "Twelve Angry Men," with team discussion afterward.

10. **Q.** *What if members won't agree to work on conflicts because they don't like the idea of conflict?*

 A. Sometimes a semantic change—restating something as a challenge rather than a conflict—will help. Other times, breaking the conflict into smaller problems helps it look less formidable. Sometimes people are simply resisting change, and you will have to stay firm and committed in your resolve to get through the issues to the other side.

 Other times it's helpful to suggest to team members that every time they shoot one idea down, they have to bring forth a new idea of their own.

 Over time team members learn that conflict is a natural and acceptable part of coexisting with other people when we treat them as equal, active partners.

11. **Q.** *What if conflicts surface lots of old issues or personality conflicts?*

 A. Conflicts usually do surface lots of old issues. We call these old issues "stamps." For example, most people have experienced temporary interpersonal conflicts that at the time they considered to be no big deal. Rather than say anything to the person, they licked an imaginary stamp and stored it in an imaginary book of prior injustices. After a while some people develop bulging books containing all the "bad" things that other people have done to them over an entire work history. These stamps are the seedbed for much of the conflict on teams.

 We knew a supervisor who manipulated the productivity on his line for ten years as revenge against a plant manager who supposedly had called him a wimp when someone recommended his name for a safety team. The plant manager had no recollection of the incident, but it was constantly on the supervisor's mind.

Luckily, we have found that all the "stamps" don't need to come flying out. Just a few important ones need to get said directly to the person involved.

12. **Q.** *Do team members really respect a team disciplinary process?*

    A. Yes, peer approval and/or rejection have tremendous power over behavior. We are group-living beings who have succeeded by complying with group norms. Having a group of people upset with us is very distressing for most people.

    The harder issue is whether a team will take the strong stand of disciplining its members. Our experience suggests that self-directed discipline does not occur until the team has matured in its interpersonal skills and has built adequate trust among its members.

13. **Q.** *Where does the traditional disciplinary process fit in with the team process?*

    A. We recommend that the team have first crack at fixing its own problems. At the point where someone isn't listening to the team or respecting the team's decision or has begun to repeat the problem, then it's important to bring in the disciplinary process of the organization.

14. **Q.** *What is the biggest behavioral hurdle for a team?*

    A. People struggle most with the concept of interdependence—the realization that what we're trying to accomplish won't happen without everyone's commitment. Theoretically, everyone says, "Sure, I know we have to work together." But members demonstrate through their behavior their opposition to working through a problem to consensus, sharing previously private information, pitching in, or scheduling meetings when everyone can attend—though these are all behaviors that symbolize an appreciation and recognition of the importance of interdependence.

15. **Q.** *Why do we struggle with the idea of interdependence?*

    A. Even though we have been group-living creatures since the beginning of human existence, we often don't trust that others will be there when we need them. So we learn to go it alone, trying to control everything as best we can—the pioneering spirit. In today's global culture, we soon realize we can't do it all; this is the moment when we recognize the need to depend on others. However, the fear and the need to control still exist.

Notes

1. M. R. Weisbord, *Productive Workplaces: Organizing and Managing for Dignity, Meaning, and Community* (San Francisco: Jossey-Bass, 1987).
2. B. Hughes, "25 Stepping Stones for Self-Directed Work Teams," *Training* (December 1991).

Chapter 4

Problems of Fear and Control

During the process of transforming a collection of people into well-functioning teams, the organization and the individuals within it will struggle with many different fears and issues of control. Often on the surface we see just symptoms: lack of participation in team meetings, withholding of information, failure to complete assignments, monopolizing a discussion, griping, and negativity. Underneath, at a deeper level, members are struggling with the requirements and the expectations of a dramatically new culture.

Basic Assumptions About People

A traditional culture makes assumptions about people on the basis of *fear*. It assumes that people: Q&A #8

- Must be told what to do and should be expected to follow
- Need discipline to follow rules
- Are motivated by money
- Need structure in order to conform
- Are lazy by nature
- Are careless and forgetful
- Are disrespectful of authority when its back is turned
- Are replaceable and expendable
- Are dishonest when tempted

- Are full of self-importance
- Are not willing to take responsibility for themselves
- Are not able to learn from mistakes
- Are limited in their capabilities
- Are lucky to have a job
- Are not capable of understanding complex business data
- Are stingy and interested only in what's in it for them

A team culture, on the contrary, makes assumptions about people on the basis of *trust*. It assumes that people are:

- Honest and trustworthy; a valuable resource
- Eager to be treated with dignity and respect
- Eager to achieve their full potential
- Willing to work hard; purposeful
- Interested in the purpose of their work and the goals of the organization they serve; curious
- Able to take a strong hand in determining what to do and how to do it
- Able to be accountable for results
- Eager to be recognized and rewarded for their achievements
- Responsive to positive leadership based on purpose
- Able to learn from their mistakes
- In favor of justice and fairness for all
- Confident in a company that is open and frank
- Generous and willing to forgive
- Unlikely to resist changes they have helped develop

During the training of a group of team leaders, two delivery men came in to the cafeteria with new glass-encased bulletin boards. As they started to hang the bulletin boards, one of the team leaders noticed that there was a lock in the center of each sliding glass frame. "How can we say we're a team and that we trust people and then lock our bulletin boards?" he asked the team. The members struggled for a few minutes, with some members expressing the "old culture" belief that posters and notices would be stolen or written on if left accessible. They soon realized the importance of making a very new and different statement and decided as a team to tell the workmen to stop putting up the bulletin boards.

These team leaders took their learning one step further and systematically examined every part of their environment to see where there was incongruence between what they were saying and what the environment was saying. They found the following: locked toolboxes and supply cabinets, locks on the locker doors, offices for management on the top floor while manufacturing was on the bottom floor, doors with locks on them, a time clock, posted company rules, a glass window in front of the receptionist's desk—and the list went on and on.

The "Muck in the Middle"

As teams move from the traditional culture to the new culture, they experience what we call "the muck in the middle." The muck in the middle is characterized by:

- Performance anxiety and apprehension
- Trial runs with many mistakes
- Cautious exploration of new concepts
- Efforts to glimpse and to assess what others are doing
- Strong resistance to change
- Tension, stress, short tempers
- A sense that everything is falling apart and out of control

The muck in the middle represents success, even though it doesn't look or feel like it. The muck increases as decisions get tougher, roles and responsibilities get more confusing, and members begin to experience the pain of being required to change old habits and behaviors. The team is on the move, and all types of feelings are being expressed verbally and nonverbally, consciously and subconsciously.

Feelings as Motivators

Team members must have permission to express their feelings as they progress on the cultural continuum. There are some basic rules about feelings:

- Feelings are not good or bad, they just are. Team members are encouraged to acknowledge the legitimacy of feelings.
- Emotions are the root of motivation; feelings are the root of emotion.
- If you cap feelings, you cap emotion; if you cap emotion, you cap motivation.
- Successful teams achieve a balance between completing tasks and developing relationships, which includes expressing feelings.
- Most people would rather overfunction than admit to and talk about negative feelings.
- The trust level of a team is proportional to the level of honesty about feelings.
- Different people can feel differently about the same thing.
- Telling someone how to feel about something will not affect how he or she feels; it will just make the person stop talking about the feeling.
- Most people are uncomfortable talking about feelings and need to have others take responsibility for creating a protective environment so feelings can emerge.
- People's feelings can change and perspectives can shift for no obvious reason.

Most of the feelings that surface during the muck in the middle have their basis in fear and issues of control.

Surfacing Fears

Q&A #1

Typical fears that can surface during transition from one culture to another include:

- *Fear of the unknown.* What will the new culture look like? How will I fit in? Will I be successful? Will we make the right choices?
- *Fear of responsibility.* Will I be able to handle the added responsibility? Do I want it? What if I make mistakes? What will happen if I let others down?
- *Fear of failure.* Will I embarrass myself in front of others?

Will I be able to learn all these new skills as fast as everyone else?

- *Fear of loss of control.* Will others be able to make wise choices? Will they know what mistakes to avoid? Can I live with the results of their choices?
- *Fear of rejection.* What will my old friends think? What if the team doesn't like me? What if members laugh at my ideas?
- *Fear of success.* How will this change my life and thinking if it's successful? Can I handle all this demand? Will more be added on if I prove myself capable? How will people act at home?
- *Fear of change.* Will I become a different person? How will my friends and family react to the new me? Will I lose all that I used to be? Will people remember why they hired me?
- *Fear of abandonment.* What if I'm left out here all alone? What if it begins to really matter to me?

Fear is a natural response to any environmental condition that we believe threatens our well-being. Our prehuman response system goes into action, and we decide between a "fight" and a "flight" response to the condition. The assertive, rational response must be learned.

Using Fear to Resist Change

Q&A #5

When a team focuses too much on its fear and loses its ability to get work done, the members may be using fear to resist an impending change. At that point the team should ask: (1) What fears are we able to do something about? (2) What fears are out of our control? (3) How will we let go of the ones out of our control?

A team that was crippled by fear because of past organizational decisions found it helpful to write out all its fears on a piece of flip-chart paper. Then they folded it up, put it in a shoe box, and put the box on the shelf. When someone brought up one of the fears during discussion, they were able to say, "Yup, we've got that one up there."

Reducing Supervisors' Fears

Most supervisors are promoted to their positions because they have a proven track record of doing a job well. Few supervisors have the people skills required to coach and motivate without special training. Add to this reality the extra demands of building a team, and you can see why the supervisor is properly anxious. In addition, organizations often make it clear that the introduction of teams will mean the elimination of supervisory positions. Special sensitivity should be shown to the following points:

- Supervisors' fears are valid and deserve open, honest discussion with the team and management.
- Most teams believe—in error—that they don't need their supervisors. If put to the test, it will not take long for them to realize otherwise.
- Supervisors need assurance that a job still exists for them as defined in revised job descriptions that explain the requirements of their new role. A manager mentor can be particularly helpful for a supervisor in this transition phase.
- Supervisors are human beings with feelings, not filing cabinets that can simply be moved two doors down. New team members may need to be reminded of the code of conduct so that hurtful things are not said to or about the supervisor.
- Supervisors should be actively involved in creating the hand-off plan (a list of all the supervisor's tasks and a schedule for when the team might take on the tasks), particularly for self-directed teams. They can also facilitate defining the new working relationship of the team with other departments.
- Supervisors are typically task-oriented individuals who do better when given specific tasks to help the team in the beginning, rather than vague instructions about building relationships.

Understanding Management Fears

While supervisors fear their jobs will be eliminated, managers most often fear that their job responsibilities will be increased. Whereas once they were responsible for a single department, now they might oversee teams from three or four different work areas. New skill development must occur in the areas of communication, listening, tolerance and patience, time management, willingness to let go in incremental steps, and acceptance that there is no magic bullet that will set the team straight tomorrow.

Building Trust

Q&A #7, 11

When an organization downsizes staff or discharges an employee, fear will reassert itself on the team. An open discussion to sort out facts from feelings, assumptions, and expectations will help diminish the fear. However, it is naive to think that these types of negative decisions will not have an impact. No team operates in a vacuum. When loss of any sort is felt, either directly or indirectly, the team will need time to regain its balance and direction.

The opposite of fear for a team is trust. In 1967, Douglas McGregor defined trust as "the knowledge that you will not deliberately or accidentally, consciously or unconsciously, take unfair advantage of me. I can put my situation at the moment, my status and self-esteem in this group, our relationship, my job, my career, even my life, in your hands with complete confidence."[1]

Our level of trust—whether open and spontaneous, hesitant and cautious, or nonexistent—is based on whether we perceive a balance between what we are giving to the situation and what we are getting from it.[2] If team members see a balance between what they give and get, their trust level will be high.

A participant once shared another insight on trust with us. We were doing the trust fall exercise, and we asked the team members what made them able to let go and fall backwards. Most replied, "I knew the person would catch me." Another participant then added, "Even if the person didn't catch me, I trusted myself enough to know I could deal with the consequences if I landed on the floor."

How Trust Breaks Down on a Team

- Team members fail to deliver on promises or complete assignments or make empty promises.
- Team members have hidden expectations about what will or won't be achieved.
- Members talk about each other outside meetings.
- Members do not surface problems when they occur but instead collect injustices.
- Management and others give the team a reward that has no value to some team members.
- Team members have hidden agendas that involve control and manipulation.
- Members experience a lack of communication, finding out something after the general public knows.
- Members delegate responsibility without authority.
- Members form cliques and subgroups.
- There is competition among teams in the same organization.

The more distrust exists on the team, the more each member will need to feel in control and will see the lack of trust as a threat of varying degree.[3]

A threat represents the potential for loss of control—perhaps a threat to entitlement or an infringement on spare time. To reduce the threat, team members may exert their power in a number of ways.

Types of Power

- *Real and appropriate power.* Power that has openly and legitimately been given the individual by the team (example: facilitator, process observers, timekeeper)
- *Expert power.* Power that comes as a result of the team member's skill, expertise, and experience (example: subject matter expert)
- *Position power.* Power that comes from a title or authority a

team member has on the outside (example: CEO, department head, supervisor)

- *Self-esteem power.* Power that comes from the team member's inner confidence and belief in oneself (example: intelligent and articulate speaker, straight shooter)
- *Competitive power.* Power that comes from beating an opponent by being more verbally or physically aggressive (example: talking over someone during debate, using "you" statements to accuse)
- *Guilt power.* Power that comes by making others feel guilty for what they have or haven't done (example: blaming others, mentioning the amount of work/effort given)

Power is a subtle force in a group of people. The tiniest behaviors do not go unnoticed; pushing back a chair and crossing one's arms during discussion, frowning, taking phone calls, and name dropping are all behaviors that are received and processed by the brain to form a picture of the power distribution among team members.

We often think of power as an aggressive behavior. However, there are many passive techniques for exerting power on a team. The most common one involves a member who suggests that he or she "just can't get the hang of team building" as a way to excuse any bad behavior. We call this Victim Power.

Relinquishing Control

The more control a person has in the organization, the more power that person will have to relinquish to be an effective team member. For a company president, relinquishing control means deliberately holding back her or his point of view and allowing the team to spend time searching for the right answer, rather than providing it for them, and doing some of the routine maintenance tasks.

Who Must Relinquish Control?

Q&A #3

- The CEO who has functioned as the organization's parent and who tends to micromanage his or her employees in a wide variety of areas

- The department head who has always led every staff meeting and approved every decision
- The supervisor who has always assigned the tasks, scheduled orders, and fixed others' mistakes
- Employees who have previously relied on their connections with influential people for preferred status

The line supervisor and the middle manager often experience the greatest difficulty with loss of control. Their jobs have always required them to exert control; now the opposite is being required. Without proper training they are often totally lost.

Three Ways Members Resist Relinquishing Control

1. Members may detach from the team in order to maintain their "old" power and control by:
   - Threatening to quit
   - Not participating or volunteering
   - Blaming others
   - Walking away
   - Suggesting that team building is a passing fancy
   - Being very busy with their own tasks
   - Experiencing increased absences/sickness
2. Members may be slow and reluctant to give up old ways of doing things and delay their own effort or debate pros and cons for long periods of time by:
   - Suggesting that a manager or supervisor just wants to do his or her job
   - Not volunteering
   - Holding back until a decision is almost in place
   - Having a rejection reaction: "You didn't include me, so I won't participate"
   - Stating that the teamwork is "too much"
   - Maintaining tunnel vision
   - Procrastinating
   - Discounting the contribution of others
   - Viewing team building and work as separate things
3. Members may actively look for ways to prevent or sabotage the team by:

- Stating that team building is not part of the job
- Calling team building a waste of time
- Suggesting that things are worse than ever
- Telling others that "we'll be sorry we ever did this"
- Remarking that the boss or owner will probably do what he or she wants anyway
- Expressing hopelessness
- Attacking customers in the name of team building

Magazine articles often say, "And then Company A formed a team" or "The A team reached a decision." We have never known it to be that easy. We are convinced that the variety of behaviors in the human repertoire for asserting or avoiding control is endless. We encourage teams to put these items on the agenda on a regular basis. Even if everyone is practicing denial at a particular meeting ("What! I've never been controlling"), if the topic comes up often enough, sooner or later someone will take a risk and speak the truth.

Overcoming Resistance

The Team's Role in Overcoming Resistance

- Understand and discuss the resistance openly among members; acknowledge feelings
- Anticipate and plan for the resistance; set up mechanisms to identify it
- Convert the resistance to positive support
- Educate team members, and develop diagnostic skill
- Comfort members without trying to "fix" their discomfort
- Discipline members when necessary, and define the consequences for breaking the team's rules
- Promote gains (benefits) for both the individual and the team

There is a point when a team shifts from a collection of individuals to an entity that is greater than its parts—what's commonly called synergy. The team takes control of its actions and behaviors, and its power then exceeds that of all its individual members combined.

A team is ready to assert control when:

- Trust level among members is high and spontaneous.
- Expectations are realistic and defined.
- Members are willing to accept peer pressure as a way of controlling the team.
- Members are committed to succeeding as a team.
- Benefits are clear and defined.
- Members are able to handle both process issues and task issues.
- Members are mature and patient.

QUESTIONS AND ANSWERS: How to Eliminate Problems of Fear and Control

1. **Q.** *Does fear always exist during the team building process?*

   A. Every team member experiences fear at some point in the team building process. For hourly employees, the fear is often greatest in the beginning. Suddenly they are thrust into meetings where they are expected to have ideas, speak out on issues, and reach conclusions. It's a foreign land for line staff.

   The fear for managers usually surfaces when the team is about to make its first important decision. The manager has to let go and let it happen and not interfere or try to "fix it" so everything comes out perfectly.

   Perhaps the supervisor experiences more fear than any other staff member. A well-functioning team doesn't need a supervisor as defined in the past, and it doesn't take long for the supervisor to know it. Unless the supervisor is actively redefining his or her role with the team and has strong support from upper management, the relationship between the team and the supervisor becomes extremely strained, as both play tug-of-war for the same authority and responsibility.

2. **Q.** *Do some people disguise their fear?*

   A. All of us disguise our fear from time to time. In fact, it's rare for someone to say, "I'm really scared about . . ." Instead, we do all kinds of other behaviors: procrastinate, worry, use guilt, blame others, demand perfection.

3. **Q.** *Are certain personalities more controlling than others?*

   A. Instead of thinking of one personality as more controlling than another, it may be helpful to recognize that different personalities have different ways of controlling. For example, an extrovert may control by talking to ten people about a subject and getting the team all stirred up; an introvert, on the other hand, may withdraw and sulk in his office and make other team members feel uncomfortable and guilty.

   A personality style that uses intellect more than feelings will rely on exhaustive research, data, and logic to try to control a situation. On the other hand, the feeler personality style will focus more on the impact of the situation on relationships. A results-oriented personality style will control by setting up a competition (e.g., "We can beat them if we do it my way"), while the intuitive personality style will simply generate more and more ideas until one clicks with the team.

   Every team benefits from a mix of personality styles and, in fact, must learn to value diversity as part of its growth process.

4. **Q.** *Can personality conflicts ruin a team?*

   A. If members are unable to get past their personality differences (e.g., I like participatory discussion; he likes giving orders), it will be extremely difficult for the team to agree on a common goal and move forward.

   Interestingly, we have found some of the most difficult personality conflicts to resolve are those among older women employees who were taught all their lives to smile graciously and not say anything negative. So while they have lots of complaints, they wouldn't dream of voicing them directly to the person involved. However, that doesn't prevent them from talking to others or periodically uttering a "sotto voce" snipe.

5. **Q.** *How do most employees resist the change to team building?*

   A. Typically, resistance falls into two categories: overt and covert. The overt resister comes to training and repeatedly interrupts to suggest that whatever is being taught won't work (e.g., meetings don't work, consensus won't work, finding a common goal won't work, and so on). When the overt resister does role play, he or she typically tries to turn it into a joke or gives such short answers that the situation dies on the vine. Once the team is formed, the overt resister is typically quite vocal in meetings, often using "plosives" (e.g., "Yeah, right! I don't believe this!") to state negative opinions.

   The covert resister, on the other hand, never openly demonstrates any problem with teams and, in fact, is often publicly supportive. Behind the scenes, though, a different opinion emerges. The covert resister has such a busy schedule that he or she has no time for team meetings, often remains mute during the meetings he or she attends, hides behind an "I didn't know we agreed to do that" victim stance, and does absolutely nothing to promote team building in his or her own department.

6. **Q.** *What are the best ways to break through all these behavior styles?*

   A. Experts disagree here. Some say to put all your energy on the team champions and forget the rest—sooner or later they'll come along or leave. Others say to surface the issues and bring behaviors out into the open.

   Part of the problem, we believe, is that both the covert and the overt resisters are playing by old performance standards, where collaboration and effective communication are not measured in any real terms.

   The most effective means we have seen for bringing behavior in line is to state clearly the desired behavior and the consequences that will occur if that behavior is not demonstrated. For example, suppose the team manager becomes aware that the overt resister is doing serious damage to the early morning team meeting. Immediately, the team manager meets with the resister, asks about the problem, and provides guidelines for acceptable behaviors to resolve the problem. The team manager notes that the behavior being used is not acceptable and must change immediately. The team manager can use the same process to handle the covert resister, even though the behavior may be more difficult to identify.

This means of intervention puts pressure on the team and the team manager to identify desirable and undesirable behaviors and the consequences for each.

Often, however, we have seen the reverse occur. Management, supervisors, and even team leaders are intimidated by the overt resister and try to appease, humor, or ignore him or her. The resister—perhaps enjoying center stage or maybe just sensing ambivalence—is strengthened in his or her behavior by this approach.

7. **Q.** *Can fear be a positive motivator?*

A. Kathleen Ryan and Daniel Oestreich have written an excellent book called *Driving Fear Out of the Workplace,*[4] in which they state that 50 percent of the people surveyed said that fear is not a positive motivator. Another 10 percent said fear is a positive motivator only when it is self-imposed.

Sometimes we have seen managers use fear to bring in line a team that is suggesting changes of which the managers do not approve. The managers let it be known that they aren't happy with the proposed changes and that something should be "done" to those who suggested the changes. It doesn't take long for the reaction to filter back to the team and for the team to react to the fear. Here fear is serving as a motivator of behavior.

The trouble with using fear as a motivator is that people usually dislike people who make them fearful and will scheme in countless ways to get even. As a consequence, tremendous energy (individual and collective) is wasted on negative scheming, rather than being used for productive teamwork.

8. **Q.** *What about a team that uses fear and an unwillingness to accept criticism as a smokescreen behind which to hide other problems?*

A. People have learned that one effective way to function in our society is to play the victim. This style is epitomized by the team member who says, "You go ahead and make the decision. You lost me hours ago." What a great way to let yourself off the hook!

One team we have worked with has, on occasion, made the president of the organization the symbolic ogre, despite the fact that he has never fired anyone. They transfer ownership and power to him as a way of avoiding responsibility for their own behavior.

We've found that the best solution is to discuss openly fear and how various team members respond to it, without throwing any fear-inducing statements into the process. If hot tempers are a problem, it's best to hire an impartial facilitator to guide team discussion.

9. **Q.** *What can you do about a manager who is very inconsistent and who adds to everyone's level of fear?*

A. Most people agree that they would rather work for a totally autocratic boss—and know exactly what to expect—than work for someone who is inconsistent.

Employees who work for inconsistent bosses usually have numerous systems in place to read the boss's mood at key times during the day. The most common question is often "How's his mood today?" Everything the staff does or says is in response to the boss's mood.

A technique for working with an inconsistent individual is to suggest that you have the problem. For example, you might say, "I must have missed something because I thought you said *X* and then I heard you say *Y*. I must not have been paying attention." Other times it is helpful simply to have another team member validate your observation that the person is inconsistent and will probably not change.

10. **Q.** *What happens when feelings aren't expressed openly on a team?*

    A. It's no wonder we have trouble talking about our feelings. For years we have been told to leave our feelings and problems at the door before we come to work. Most of us have worked out other methods for dealing with our negative feelings, ranging from exercise and good friendships to the less productive remedies of eating, drinking, and insomnia.

    When people don't express their feelings to other team members, the feelings don't go away. Usually the feelings are directed inward for a time while we beat ourselves up for being so stupid or whatever; then the feelings get directed outward again—usually at someone who is "littler" than we are. By the time the feelings come out again, we often don't associate them with what originally made us angry.

    The more feelings remain unexpressed on a team, the more energy will be devoted toward something other than the team's goal.

11. **Q.** *What components must be included in a trusting environment?*

    A. So many things combine to create an overall impression of a trusting environment: (1) the free flow of communication and information (when people are in the information loop, they feel included and valued); (2) the practice of treating others with respect and common courtesy; (3) the valuing of feedback (whether good or bad) as a gift, because I could choose to keep you in the dark and talk behind your back; and (4) efforts to make people feel as secure as possible and not deliberately to encourage anxiety or fear.

12. **Q.** *What one thing do you tell teams more often than anything else in relationship to fear and control?*

    A. We remind team members to "cut each other some slack." People can be very hard on each other, often appearing to relish finding one another's mistakes.

When teams are in the second stage of development, the infighting can become quite vicious. Giving someone the benefit of the doubt can go a long way toward rebuilding strained relationships. Teams flourish in a blamefree environment.

13. **Q.** *How does entitlement impact team building and the fear issue?*

    A. Entitlement is the word used to describe the organizational practice of providing so many benefits that the members begin to think the benefits are owed to them. The team building culture, to the contrary, requires employees to take responsibility and to contribute actively to the organization's well-being. Entitlement and team building are two different worlds. According to Judith Bardwick, author of *Danger in the Comfort Zone,*[5] you cannot pass from entitlement to a greater level of responsibility and risk-taking without experiencing fear.

14. **Q.** *How do you balance the benefit of requiring higher performance standards with the fear that results?*

    A. This is where the manager and the supervisor are crucial to the process as coaches. They are the key players in convincing team members that, although the performance standards have increased, the team has the skill, ability, and commitment to perform at the required level.

Notes

1. D. McGregor, *The Professional Manager* (New York: McGraw-Hill, 1967).
2. R. Huseman and J. Hatfield, *Managing the Equity Factor* (Boston: Houghton Mifflin, 1989).
3. *Whitewater: A Teambuilding Simulation* (Ann Arbor, Mich.: Orion, 1987).
4. K. D. Ryan and D. K. Oestreich, *Driving Fear Out of the Workplace* (San Francisco: Jossey-Bass, 1991).
5. J. M. Bardwick, *Danger in the Comfort Zone* (New York: AMACOM, 1991).

Chapter 5

Team Decision Making and Problem Solving

The results of extensive research indicate that collective decision making is a more productive process than individual decision making (Mayo, 1933; Likert, 1961; Argyris, 1971; Lorsch and Lawrence, 1972; Jewell and Reitz, 1981; and McGregor, 1985).

Benefits of Team Decision Making

Q&A #10, 16

- New and different ideas emerge.
- Understanding and support increase.
- Individual points of view are aired and reconciled.
- Self-interests are surfaced and incorporated into decisions.
- Strong commitment to the decision develops.
- Increased learning and personal growth occur.
- Intellectual competence is enhanced.
- Increased awareness and empathy for the decision-making process are created.
- No winners or losers emerge; therefore, there is greater unity among team members.
- Team members are persuaded, rather than coerced.
- More opinions and viewpoints are expressed.
- The importance of each member's view is confirmed.
- Backroom politics are discouraged.
- More thought and energy are required than for a simple vote.

Q&A #1,2,13

Conditions Required for Effective Problem Solving

- An attitude of scientific exploration
- A passion for data and choices
- Willingness to talk about experiences
- Willingness and ability to listen
- Belief that conflict is vital to good decisions
- Ego strength and confidence to accept member challenges
- Refusal to use power as a problem-solving tool
- Willingness to encourage and support team members
- Self-discipline to avoid extraneous and repetitive discussion

Gathering Ideas

Four different techniques are useful for generating ideas on a team. They are brainstorming, brainwriting, the Affinity Diagram, and the Delphi Method.

Q&A #6

1. Brainstorming

- Decide what topic you want to discuss.
- Take turns giving ideas about the topic.
- Record each idea on a list that everyone can see using a flip chart or a blackboard.
- Hold comments and criticisms about ideas until after the session.
- Keep the tempo moving with an "anything goes" attitude.
- Allow only one idea per turn.
- Permit members to pass if they have no idea to give during a turn.
- Keep on taking ideas until everyone has said "pass" or until it's time for the brainstorming session to end.

Below are some ideas that are useful for enhancing a brainstorming session:

Change: How might a characteristic of something (either product or process) be changed or modified?

Multiply:	Think of how something would be if it were larger.
Subtract:	Think of how something would be if it were smaller.
Substitute.	Think of how something could be used in place of something else.

2. *Brainwriting*

Brainwriting[1] is particularly helpful when members are not comfortable with the speed of brainstorming or when the issue carries some conflict.

Here's an example of how brainwriting works. A team of real estate agents was struggling with the problem of vacation scheduling. The agents had spent several hours going around and around listening to each person's point of view but getting no closer to a solution. Brainwriting allowed them to focus on the question "How can we solve the vacation schedule problem?" They generated more than twenty-five ideas in ten minutes and reached a solution by multivoting (described in this chapter) to determine which choices everyone liked best.

- Distribute a piece of paper with twenty-one squares (seven rows of squares with three per column) on it to each member.
- Have each member write down three ideas and put the paper in a center pool.
- Ask each member to draw a new paper from the pool and add three more ideas that are either new or expansions of ideas a team member has already put on the form.
- Exchange papers until each member's form is nearly full.
- Have members read aloud in a round robin the ideas on the forms (members should cross out ideas that are repeated on their own form).

Ten minutes of brainwriting with ten people usually generates seventy-five to one hundred ideas.

Figure 5-1 contains the form to use in this process.

Figure 5-1. Brainwriting form.

1	2	3
4	5	6
7	8	9
10	11	12
13	14	15
16	17	18
19	20	21

3. The Affinity Diagram

An Affinity Diagram is particularly useful when a team wants to generate ideas and group or order them according to some organizing principle. Affinity is very effective with larger groups or when the topic offers a wide variety of choices that require grouping. For example, a diverse team might be discussing improvements in customer service. The discussion grows disjointed, with lots of ideas flying in different directions, many apparently at odds with one another. An Affinity Diagram can help organize the discussion.

Follow these steps to create an Affinity Diagram:

- *Capture all ideas.* The team states the topic (e.g., improvements to customer service) and writes down its ideas, each one on a separate slip of paper.
- *Group all ideas.* The slips are spread out on a table or put on a wall. In silence, team members move them around and arrange them into related groupings.
- *Look for patterns.* The team talks about why items were grouped together and the patterns that are apparent.

There are several benefits to using the Affinity Diagram:

- It's simple and quick. A team can group random ideas in a short time (ten to fifteen minutes).
- It allows people to discover patterns on their own.
- It moves a team toward consensus.
- It builds in ownership of the results.

4. The Delphi Method

- Each team member independently and anonymously writes down comments and suggestions about ways to deal with a problem or issue.
- Ideas are compiled, reproduced, and distributed to team members for observation and reaction.
- Each member provides feedback to the entire team concerning each of the comments and proposed solutions.

- The members reach consensus on which solution is most acceptable to the team as a whole.

One of the greatest benefits of creating teams is the vast amount of ideas that can be generated by individual members and by the team members functioning synergistically. The best teams use brainstorming (or a variation of it) on a constant basis.

Team members "grow into" the idea generation process. They may have stopped sharing ideas because of negative responses from a supervisor or manager and may need to test the water some with fairly benign ideas before they feel comfortable taking any significant risk.

Prioritizing Ideas

There are several techniques for narrowing ideas into priorities. They include multivoting and the Nominal Group Technique.

Q&A #7

Multivoting

Multivoting is used to narrow the number of items for consideration.

1. Each person on the team votes for as many ideas as he or she likes.
2. The ideas that get the most votes are circled.
3. The remaining ideas are consolidated where possible.
4. Each person votes again, but this time for only half the number of ideas that are circled.
5. Multivoting continues until the list is down to at least three but no more than five ideas.

Nominal Group Technique (NGT)

The Nominal Group Technique tries to provide a way to give everyone in the team an equal voice in problem selection. It is called nominal group because of the limited discussion and participation involved in the procedure. The steps in the process are as follows:

1. Team members write (or say) the problems and put them on flip-chart sheets that everyone can see.
2. The team consolidates similar problem statements into single items.
3. Team members write on a piece of paper letters corresponding to the number of problem statements the team produced. For example, if there are four problem statements, everyone writes the letters A through D on the paper.
4. The team leader makes sure that each problem statement has a letter in front of it and then asks the team members to vote on which problem they consider most important by putting a 4 next to that problem's letter. For example, the problem list might look like this:

A. Customer complaints

B. Poor communication

C. Slow software

D. No policies

Each member's paper will look like this:

A. __________

B. __________

C. __________

D. __________

If someone thinks "poor communication" is the number-one problem, that person's paper will look like this:

A. __________

B. 4

C. __________

D. __________

Everyone completes the list by voting what's second-most important, third-most important, and so on. Here is another person's list of rated items:

A. 2
B. 1
C. 3
D. 4

5. The team may decide to use an alternate ranking approach that involves the "one-half plus one" rule. This rule suggests ranking only one half of the items plus one. For example, if thirty items were generated, team members would rate only sixteen ideas.
6. Team members add up the number of points for each line. The item with the highest number is the most important one to the total team. In this case "C" (slow software) is the most important item, with a total of fourteen points.

A. **2,3,2,4,1 = 12**
B. **1,4,2,3,1 = 11**
C. **3,1,3,3,4 = 14**
D. **4,2,4,1,2 = 13**

7. The team puts the whole list in priority order and begins with item one and works through the list.

A. **C**
B. **D**
C. **A**
D. **B**

Analyzing Ideas

Process Flowcharting

Sometimes team members need to examine how a particular task is completed or why a particular problem is occurring. Any process, no matter how small or complex, can be flowcharted using the symbols shown in Figure 5-2.

Figure 5-2. A symbolic representation of process flowcharting.

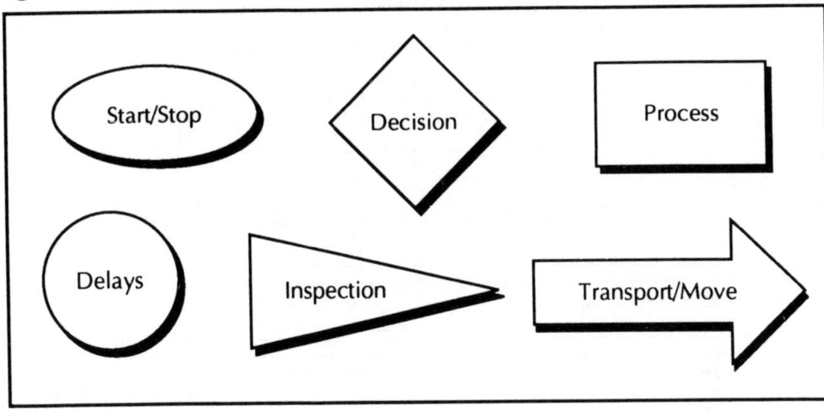

It's often helpful to have the team members compare their individual charts. More often than not, valuable information emerges about how each person handles a particular process and how he or she assumes that others handle it.

Process flowcharting can help teams understand where bottlenecks exist in a particular process, improve discussion by focusing the entire team on key steps in the process, and encourage a scientific, impartial approach to problem solving.

Figure 5-3 is an example of a full-fledged process flowchart, illustrating how to proceed if the answer to a particular question is *yes* or *no*.

In the beginning, team members, especially those who are more concerned about results than process, may struggle with the step-by-step detail of a process flowchart.

Collecting Data

Team problem solving and decision making must include collecting and presenting data to the team itself or to other teams. Sometimes simple charts are sufficient, especially charts that identify how many times the problem occurs, what type of problem occurs most often, what times of day the problem occurs, and where the problem occurs. Team members are encouraged to

Figure 5-3. Sample process flowchart.

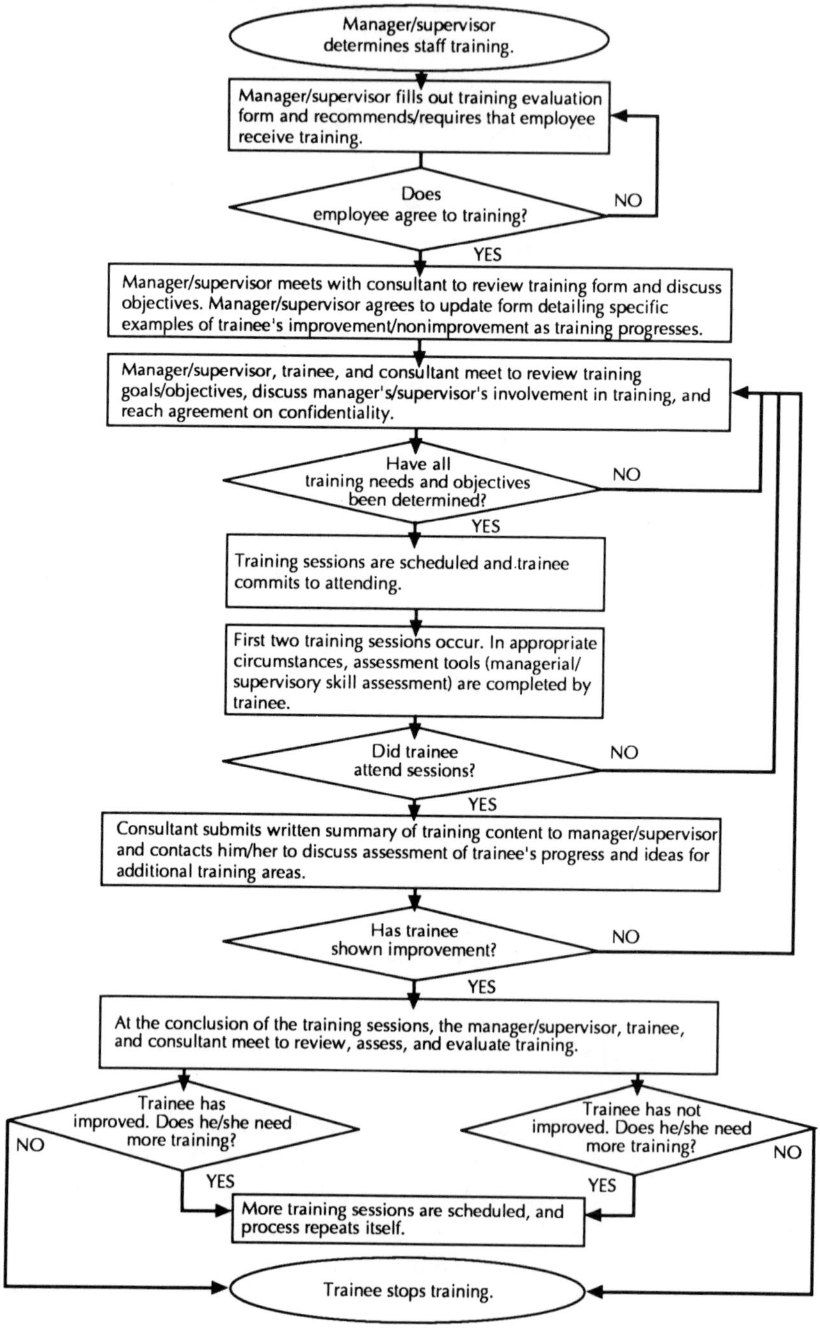

make simple pencil-and-paper charts and to share even preliminary results with other members. However, this type of thinking is difficult for most American adults and requires that all team members be trained in similar skils.

Pareto Charts

One of the most effective ways to summarize and illustrate data is through the use of a Pareto chart. A Pareto chart puts items in descending order with the sum of all items equaling 100 percent (see Figure 5-4). The points in the graph indicate how the sum of 100 is arrived at by the accumulation of all five percentages.

For example, one team member was responsible for putting together all the data from a staff survey and presenting the results to the entire staff. He began by setting up simple response charts and putting a hash mark for each response. Then he totaled the responses and put them into a Pareto chart that made it crystal clear which problems had priority among the staff. The simple presentation was clear and effective and had full support of the staff within minutes.

Figure 5-4. A Pareto chart.

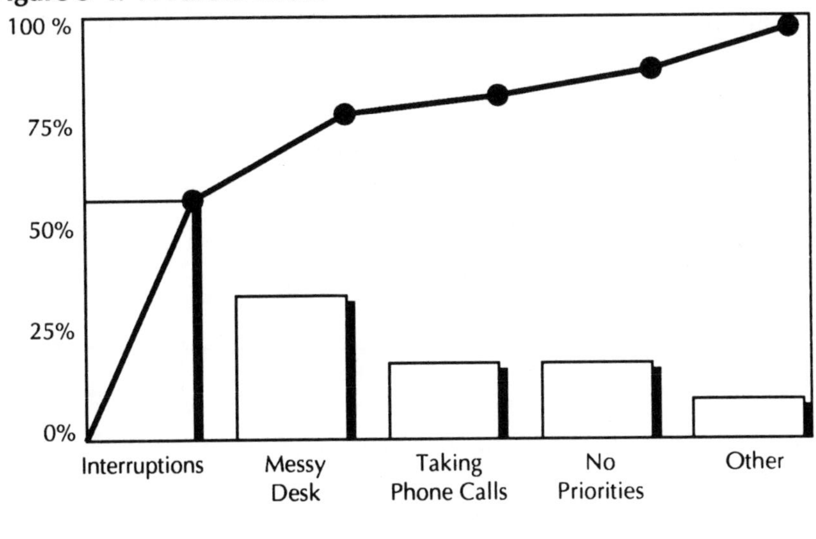

Cause-and-Effect Diagrams (Fishbones)

After the data are gathered and a single problem or issue has been isolated, the team builds a cause-and-effect diagram or fishbone that looks at six key areas: materials, machinery, methods, measurements, people, and culture (see Figure 5-5). During this process, the team brainstorms various reasons for problems in each category. Then the team identifies the main causes from all those listed. Multivoting or NGT are both effective at this point to help the team narrow and prioritize the greatest causes of the problem.

Developing Solution Alternatives

Solution Matrix

Once the team has identified its top problem and brainstormed several solution ideas, it can develop a matrix that answers the key questions that it has established as criteria for a good decision (see Figure 5-6).

Cost/Benefit Analysis

Another useful tool is to have the team complete a cost/benefit analysis by identifying all the costs related to a certain solution and all the benefits deriving from that solution (see Figure 5-7).

Figure 5-5. The cause-and-effect diagram.

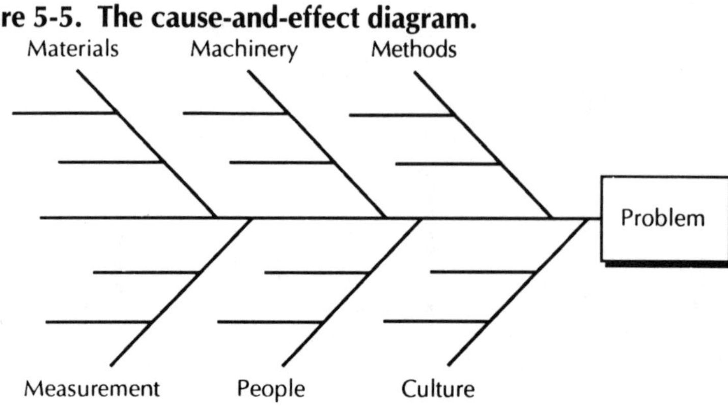

Figure 5-6. The solution matrix.

Possible Solutions	*Easy Implemen-tation*	*Cost High/Low*	*Upper Mgt. Support*	*Creates New Problems*
1				
2				
3				

Figure 5-7. The cost/benefit analysis.

Cost	Benefit

Now the team is ready to make a decision. If solid preparation has occurred, the team will have little trouble reaching a consensus because, more often than not, the solution is obvious. When teams struggle with decisions, it is usually because most of the preparatory steps have not been completed and members are trying to force a subjective decision on the group.

Making Decisions

There are a number of ways that decisions can be reached on a team. Most people are comfortable with voting (a democratic method). However, voting results in winners and losers, and losers tend to work against a goal they don't like. Therefore, we encourage teams to strive for consensus and use voting only in the early stages of problem solving to narrow choices.

Ways Teams Can Make Decisions

1. *Majority rule (voting).* Decisions are made according to a vote of a majority or a fixed percentage of members.
2. *Minority rule.* One or two members of a team or a subgroup make decisions for the entire team.
3. *Autocracy.* A decree, sanction, or order is given from a single person who has enough authority to carry it out.
4. *Autocracy with polling.* A single person with authority solicits opinions before making decisions.
5. *Decision by nondecision.* No conclusion is reached even after considerable discussion, often because the issue is too hot or because no process exists for closure.
6. *Consensus.* An entire team agrees to a best solution to which all members can commit themselves at the time.
7. *Unanimity.* Each member fully agrees to, and can fully support, the decision.

A quick way to remember the decision-making continuum is to apply it to making dinner. If a spouse decides what the family is to have for dinner, the decision is autocratic. If husband and wife decide, it's minority rule; if the family votes, it's majority rule; if there are no leftovers, the decision was by consensus.

The Decision-Making Process

The following are important criteria for an effective decision-making process.

- A clearly defined problem or issue
- Agreement on who has responsibility for making a decision about the problem or issue

- Agreement on procedures and methods to be used before discussion begins
- Clarity about the level of authority the team has to either recommend or decide
- Effective communication that generates ideas
- Data and other information to help develop objective conclusions
- Appropriate team size for decision making
- A way of deciding on the best choice
- A method for building commitment to and ownership of the decision
- Honest commitment from the organization to carry out the decision

Consensus Decision Making

Douglas Steere, author of *Quaker Spirituality,* calls consensus decision making "participative humility," perhaps because of the following three considerations:[2] Q&A #8

1. Each member must feel he or she has been heard and understood by the rest of the team.
2. Each member must be able to live with the decision or solution.
3. Each member must be willing to commit to his or her role in carrying out the decision or implementing the solution.

Our culture is not practiced in the art of consensus. Most people become very impatient with the time and energy required to look for answers that are acceptable to everyone. They would rather use majority rule and risk the noninvolvement and even potential sabotage of the minority.

The attitude and spirit of a team that has achieved consensus is markedly different from that in groups that vote. A team can "feel" consensus when it occurs, and the energy generated is well worth the struggle to achieve consensus. Not every decision made by a team, however, requires consensus.

When to Use Consensus Decision Making

- When the issue being considered is an important one and the unity gained is worth the time
- When a sense of synergy among team members is a priority
- When a number of alternatives and courses of action should be explored and considered
- When it is important to explore as many facets of an issue as possible
- When the solution to a problem creates new problems
- When the process for reaching the decision is as important as the decision itself
- When the delay caused by the process of reaching consensus will prevent the team from jumping to conclusions about a problem
- When the decision is final

Attitudes and Behaviors Required for Consensus Decision Making

- Ability to speak for oneself—"I prefer, I need"
- Enough self-discipline to stay focused on the task and process
- Clear, honest, and direct speech in terms of who, what, when, where
- Ability to restate concerns or requests as suggestions or proposals (e.g., "I have trouble with this and would feel better if we added . . .")
- Ability to determine personal preference and to state it before a team
- Ability to distinguish facts from opinions
- Ability to identify and name feelings (both one's own and others)
- Low level of defensiveness as people question ideas
- Willingness to listen; ability to process other viewpoints
- Commitment to finding the best answer
- Low level of competitiveness
- Sufficient self-esteem to be able to say no to a team

- Ability to look for mutually supported alternatives
- Listening for and synthesizing areas of agreement
- Patience to hold back from premature decision making
- Desire or curiosity to try consensus decision making

Several members of one team of well-educated people decided that the best solution was to move ahead on its task with or without the support of a larger group. When one member of the team objected, the other members said, "Well, then, let's vote." When the team member responded, "I thought teams tried to reach consensus," the other members chided him and proceeded to vote anyway. He and another member opposed the action. After the meeting, several members stopped by to tell him they agreed with his position. Question: How committed to the team do you think that member was from that point forward?

Consensus Guidelines

When a team has progressed to the point of decision making, an effective facilitator uses the following steps to help the team achieve consensus:

1. A topic or idea is placed before the team for discussion.
2. The topic is discussed; questions and concerns are raised; data and solution options are presented.
3. The team decides whether to try to achieve consensus, how long it will spend, and what it will do if consensus cannot be reached (e.g., vote, delay a decision).
4. Differences and disagreements, as well as similarities, are explored and encouraged.
5. Suggestions and modifications to the original topic are made.
6. A new idea is created by the team on the basis of the discussion.
7. The facilitator checks for consensus and sees some nonverbal cues that suggest that some members don't agree.
8. If there is no consensus, the facilitator asks for a variation of the idea and tests for consensus again. Q&A #14, 15

9. If there is still a single member who is struggling, the facilitator asks the team for "stand-aside" proposals (trial time period, modified plan).
10. If the member indicates support for a ninety-day trial period the facilitator tests for consensus again; the entire group supports the modified solution.

Sometimes people are willing to stand aside and not block consensus if certain special concessions are made. These may include:

- Not requiring the team member to work on a given task
- Recording the dissenting viewpoint in the minutes
- Stipulating that the decision does not set a precedent and therefore cannot be used as a basis for future decisions
- Setting a trial period for testing the decision and its implementation

Q&A #9

Blocking Consensus

People generally do not hold out against the weight of a team decision, even when the team is in error. The decision to block a decision is typically rare and creates considerable team tension.

Any team member who blocks a decision must have participated fully in earlier discussions. The member must consider the needs of the whole team apart from his or her individual needs and must clearly explain his or her reasons for blocking and be willing to offer compromises.

If no decision can be reached, then the team must delay resolution until more information can be gathered. A deadline for a final decision must be determined and met.

Specific Consensus Problems

1. *Two people disagree with the team.* Make sure ideas have been listened to; ask if members feel strongly enough to block. Ask if some "standing aside" options would work.
2. *Team is divided evenly.* Meet in small teams to develop proposal that everyone can live with.

3. *Pressure is being exerted on one or two people to give in.* The facilitator and/or process observers must protect participant rights to disagree.

QUESTIONS AND ANSWERS: Handling Negative Reactions to Consensus Decision Making

1. **Q.** *Why do we have such difficulty with effective problem solving?*

   A. A United States Commissioner of Education once said, "We start school as question marks and end school as periods."[3] In other words, we look for a single right answer and then stop looking as soon as we think we have it. This attitude doesn't work with team problem solving.

2. **Q.** *How have we been taught to solve problems?*

   A. That's a good question. We ask it in training, and here's what people say: Cheat, memorize, wait for the smartest person in the class to answer, think of an answer that sounds good, use an encyclopedia, ask the teacher something else and hope he or she forgets the question, ask a good friend.

   We also ask, "Where were you asked to solve problems?" Participants typically answer: in math or science. Never has anyone said English or social studies. As a consequence, we often encounter an aversion to problem solving in people who remember that they were not good students in math or science.

3. **Q.** *I can't believe you would go to so much detail to solve a simple problem. Don't most people just know what's the best decision?*

   A. Most people *think* they know the best solution, but often, after they collect their data and analyze them, they change their minds.

4. **Q.** *How do you get people to change?*

   A. Three ways: (1) by showing them how much better their decisions are when they've collected their data and used a consensus-seeking procedure, (2) by educating them with the skills to be good problem-solvers, and (3) by making quality problem solving nonnegotiable for all employees.

5. **Q.** *Doesn't the last one—making it nonnegotiable—seem pretty strong?*

   A. When something is negotiable and we don't like it, we won't even try it (witness a child with his vegetables). Certain nonnegotiables (expectations, if you will) have to be clear: We will function in teams; we will use problem-solving tools; we will make decisions by consensus; we will be required to complete necessary training.

If people sense waffling on these critical points, great amounts of time will be spent deciding, redeciding, and redeciding again.

6. **Q.** *What are the biggest problems with brainstorming?*

   A. Two problems typically emerge. Some people can't think and speak well on their feet, and they become intimidated. Brainwriting, which has members write down their ideas first, can reduce these fears considerably. The second problem is pacing. Brainstorming really should move at a very quick pace so that the wildest ideas come out. Sometimes people slow down to look for the right idea, rather than just any idea.

7. **Q.** *What do you do with the ideas that are leftover after multi-voting or NGT?*

   A. The team will need to decide whether to keep the ideas. They are sometimes a good source of creative energy for the next time around. Get people to read their list of ideas from a previous brainstorming session so that they can see how intelligent and creative they can be.

8. **Q.** *There seem to be lots of different interpretations about consensus. Would you explain them?*

   A. Consensus originated with the Quakers, and much of what is written about consensus is based on religious materials.

Some people think consensus should be the "70 percent comfortable rule," where each member is 70 percent comfortable with a decision. This concept of consensus was used with General Motors teams that manufactured the Saturn car.

One real humdinger explanation of consensus came up when a large national company instructed people who were supposedly seeking a decision by consensus to have everyone who opposed the decision leave the room so that those remaining could be in consensus. We asked what happened to the people out in the hall, and the team members said they were instructed to examine their own behavior to see why they were being disagreeable. If they opposed too many decisions, they were told, they might be asked to leave the team altogether. Obviously, this is a gross distortion of the concept of consensus.

9. **Q.** *What about when a team is going to make a wrong decision?*

A. The team member must block the decision on the grounds that he or she thinks it's wrong and can't live with the consequences of the decision. Most CEOs and senior managers do this all the time, so they don't have a lot of difficulty standing up and saying no. But it is quite another thing for an hourly employee to block a decision when a manager or the company president is in the room. The tension in the room at that moment is incredible. A team that handles the situation effectively grows tremendously through the process; suddenly, it has proof positive that conflict is okay, differences of opinion are valued, titles are meaningless, and power is based on knowledge.

10. **Q.** *What if our organization doesn't support consensus because top management thinks it takes too long?*

A. Well, we could say you might as well forget team building. But culture shifts in organizations don't always happen overnight or just as we would like them to. Try negotiation. It sounds as if time is the issue here. Ask those in charge if they will allow the team to make decisions any way it wants to as long as it doesn't take more than an agreed-upon time limit.

11. **Q.** *The skill required to achieve consensus seems to be difficult. Do you agree?*

    A. Not so much difficult as unknown. Many people have never been required to work as part of a team or to use any type of collaborative teaming skills. However, these skills can be learned, just as you can learn to play tennis or ski.

12. **Q.** *Are there any special tips?*

    A. Because so many little incidents crop up that require different thinking, we encourage team members to find mentors who are good at collaborative problem solving. Then, every time the team feels like it's at a critical juncture, it can consult a mentor or two about how to proceed. The biggest mistake is to think you know it all.

13. **Q.** *We have a couple of very bossy problem-solvers. Everything is "this isn't team and that isn't team." What should we do about these people?*

    A. It might be helpful to give the person some direct feedback (e.g., "Yesterday when we were struggling with the next step in our problem solving, I felt you cut off discussion by saying, 'Teams don't do it that way.' "). We don't recommend humor because most people miss the point that was so cleverly delivered. Sometimes it works to have two team members talk to the person. Other times, if it's just a personality quirk, ignore it and hope a more temperate tone develops as the person matures on the team.

14. **Q.** *How do you get people to let you know whether they agree or disagree?*

    A. Tell people you need a visual cue from them (e.g., head nodding, looking up and smiling) to know whether they are in agreement. Don't assume anything if you are the facilitator!

15. **Q.** *What if one or two people appear to disagree with the rest of the team? Do you ask them why?*

A. We recommend that you protect them for a time by saying something like, "I don't think we have consensus yet. Would someone like to propose a modification that might help some others come to agreement?" People have such difficulty with conflict and with being singled out that we find it helpful to encourage more discussion and then ask, "Do we now have consensus on the idea of implementing the plan in two weeks?"

We often ask to hear from people who haven't spoken in a while, hoping to pick up some of the members who are struggling with the team's idea.

The more you keep the team moving together toward a common decision, rather than pointing out the differences among individual members, the more unity and spirit will exist. More than anything, developing win-win solutions without selling the team short for a quick victory requires a commitment on the part of the facilitator and process observers.

16. **Q.** *Some say consensus is a complete waste of time. Is it?*

A. To us it's sad that people will sell themselves and each other short. The feeling that emerges after consensus is incredible—almost indescribable. People are smiling, talking freely, and their eyes are lit up. No talk occurs outside the meeting or in the halls or bathrooms, other than to work on team assignments.

Some people look at a vote and call it a victory. If only we could measure the lost energy, the decrease in motivation and drive, the bitterness and resentment, the extra time and energy spent to achieve consensus would seem cheap.

Notes

1. Brainwriting is adapted from Bernd Rohrbach, whose form appeared in B. Johannsson, *Kreativität and Marketing* (Switzerland: H. Kern, 1978).
2. D. Steere, *Quaker Spirituality* (Mahwah, N.J.: Paulist, 1984).
3. R. von Oech, *A Whack on the Side of the Head* (New York: Warner, 1983).

Chapter 6

Evaluating and Rewarding Team Performance

Several years ago a large corporation was in the process of implementing teams and sought training for its managers in team performance evaluations. However, the organization was still using a seriatim process, in which employees are ranked, to determine compensation. It wasn't surprising that employees showed no interest in working in teams when the reward system so clearly emphasized individual results.

The particular managers argued to no avail with senior managers that the evaluation and compensation systems should be changed to reflect the new team building values. Unfortunately, organizational leadership was not ready to change basic systems and structures to reflect the emphasis on team building.

Q&A #1, 9

An effective performance evaluation system recognizes and rewards what the organization values. Team functioning is based on both task completion (results) and the building of relationships (process).

Purpose of Evaluations

An evaluation system is typically designed to serve a number of different purposes:

- To motivate work performance
- To inform team members about job performance

- To clarify the job to be done
- To encourage increased competence and growth
- To enhance and improve communication
- To improve discipline and correct problem behavior/performance
- To measure performance for salary action
- To develop back-up data for management decisions (promotions, demotions, discharge)
- To encourage ownership and responsibility

It's important to remember that standard performance appraisal systems have numerous problems and are regularly under fire. For example, Total Quality Management guru W. Edwards Deming says, "The annual review of people is a major culprit generating fear and wreaking havoc in our corporations and on our people. Companies suffer untold loss because of the annual review. People emerge from their reviews shaken and destroyed, unable to function properly for months."[1] Team evaluations—so new to the scene—are likely to experience similar problems and struggles. Q&A #14

Common Problems With Traditional Performance Evaluation Systems

- Standards and ratings tend to vary widely and often unfairly, depending upon the personality of the evaluator.
- When standards are not clear, evaluators tend to reward activities rather than results.
- Employees often cannot explain the reasoning behind the rating they were given.
- Rather than surface difficulties, managers tend to give average ratings to poor performers. Q&A #13
- Managers tend to give better evaluations to employees that they like.
- Ratings often reflect general impressions, rather than specific performance.
- Managers tend to recall behavior that fits the stereotype that they have developed about the employee.
- When times are tough, managers inflate ratings to keep good employees.

- Managers often forget that the annual written evaluation is a key piece of evidence in wrongful discharge cases brought by employees.
- Evaluators are often confused whether to function as judge or coach.

Team Reviews

As a team matures, members may be asked to complete performance reviews on other members. Although the process can be intimidating for members who have never functioned as evaluators, the benefits of a team review are numerous.

Benefits of Team Reviews

- Team members know each other's performance better than managers or supervisors and can therefore evaluate one another more accurately.
- Peer pressure is a powerful motivator for team members.
- Team review solicits numerous opinions within and outside the team and is not dependent on one person's opinion.
- Team members see each other's work on a regular basis, so their observations are very accurate.
- Team evaluation supports the development of assessment skills among team members who function as evaluators.
- Members who recognize that team members will be evaluating their work show increased commitment and productivity.
- Team members become more aware of performance standards and behavior requirements because they are accountable for maintaining them.

Drawbacks of Team Reviews

- They are time-consuming.
- It is sometimes difficult to distinguish between the contributions of the team and those of individual members.

- Some members feel uncomfortable judging or evaluating other team members.
- Extensive training is required in order to become competent in giving feedback and in functioning as a performance coach.

Special Tips on Team Performance Reviews

- The review system must reinforce and support the kinds of behavior and the culture needed to implement the organization's goals (Lawler and Cohen, 1992). If the organization wants effective teams and team members, it must include team performance measures as a major part of employee reviews.
- As long as the review system rewards only job-based or task-based performance, the team will question the organization's commitment to a team culture.
- It is best to assess total team performance before having members conduct peer reviews (Mohrman, Mohrman, and Cohen, 1992).
- Team members have difficulty giving negative or constructive feedback when the evaluation is linked to other personnel decisions, such as promotions, demotions, and compensation.
- Peer reviews are best conducted when a team has reached an advanced stage of team building (Quick, 1992).
- When team members openly discuss problems they are having with other team members, they may exaggerate and generalize about the problems to gain team support. Members must actively work to avoid the bandwagon effect and maintain a level of open-mindedness.
- Teamwork can be very seductive especially for extraverts who enjoy group interaction. It's important to weigh the time spent on team tasks (e.g., 10 percent of the total job) compared to the total job and to measure accordingly.
- The review system, along with compensation systems, is often one of the last areas to change to reflect the team approach.

Types of Team Rating Systems

A person on a team actually influences three levels of job performance: the actual job he or she performs, the job he or she performs as a team member, and the team performance as it relates to the whole organization. All of these areas must be included in the review process. Most team reviews include one or more of the following rating systems to take into account the depth and breadth of the member's influence:

1. *Peer ratings.* Other members of a team assess the contribution of each team member. Individuals may accumulate a number of ratings that reflect their contributions to each project worked on.
2. *Customer satisfaction ratings.* External and internal customers rate the individual's and the team's performance.
3. *Self-appraisals.* Members of the team assess the team's performance. Q&A #6
4. *Team leader reviews.* The team leader/supervisor assesses the individual members of the team.
5. *Management reviews.* The department head evaluates individual performance with some inclusion of team results as a performance factor.

Components of an Effective Review System

Performance evaluation is but one component in a performance planning process that must include accurate job descriptions, joint goal setting, ongoing coaching, and regular and timely performance feedback.

A team evaluation must not proceed unless the following criteriA are present:

- Trust and respect between management and teams (management has to feel the team is capable of completing accurate reviews)
- Agreement about goals, procedures, and timing of the team review process

- Clear and well-defined performance objectives for the team and for individual members
- Performance measures that have been agreed to by all
- Feedback systems about team performance that provide numerous opportunities for informal assessment, coaching, and review
- Open and active exchange of information
- Methods of recognizing performance that are thoughtful and appropriate
- Respect between peers on the team

Despite the periodic grumblings of staff, the review process has always been a management function. The loss of power that accompanies a shift to team reviews will threaten any manager who has used the evaluation process as a weapon, rather than a tool.

On the other hand, managers who believe that evaluations tend to be one-sided will welcome the increased feedback from and involvement of other team members.

Performance Factors for Team Reviews

The more a team can work together to develop its own performance factors (what will be measured) and acceptable standards (the team's performance expectations), the less resistance will develop among members.

The performance evaluation tool typically describes a number of performance factors to be reviewed (e.g., quantity of work, quality of work). The list below includes team factors but also reflects level of customer satisfaction and work quality. As the team reviews and refines the factors to create its evaluation tool, it will need to define specific behaviors or results that distinguish outstanding and above average performance from average, below average, and unsatisfactory performance.

Output/Result Measures of Performance

- *Achievement of team goals.* Assistance given to the achievement of team goals; level of activity in establishing quality, efficiency, and speed of the team

- *Customer satisfaction.* Whether the member meets or exceeds customer expectations; recognizes the importance of both external/internal customers
- *Quantity of work.* Whether productivity exceeds standards without being asked; pride in workmanship, efficiency, and speed
- *Quality of work.* Performance as it relates to process control and continuous improvement; ability to perform task accurately
- *Process knowledge.* Extent of job knowledge, technical and professional skill, and ability to meet changing situations; knowledge of multiple jobs
- *Maintenance of technical systems.* Level of understanding of safety hazards, compliance with safety rules, and work habits; machinery maintenance

Input/Process Measures of Performance

With team evaluations the process measures are as important as the output/result measures. This shift from the traditional results orientation in most organizations may cause confusion and anxiety at first. In the past it might not have mattered if a supervisor yelled at an employee as long as the work got done; now the emphasis is on collaborative coaching and communicating as well as the results.

- *Support of team process.* Level of support for the use of teams to achieve goals; strong positive force in team morale; provides assistance and support of others, even under pressure
- *Participation.* Whether the member leads and participates constructively in team meetings and team tasks; actively encourages the participation of others; regularly volunteers for various team roles
- *Oral communication.* Use of open, honest, and direct communication; active listening; clarity of speech; willingness to interpret and clarify for other team members; interest in improving communication skills through giving and receiving feedback

- *Written communication.* Willingness to assist in recorder duties; ability to develop and write reports/presentations for the team
- *Collaboration and collective effort.* Level at which the member responds to others; cooperates readily with all team members; demonstrates positive attitude and support for others
- *Conflict resolution.* Sees conflict as helpful in promoting different perspectives; freely expresses views on difficult issues, including nonproductive team behaviors
- *Planning and goal setting.* Use of proactive planning and goal setting to achieve desired results; ability to be flexible in modifying plan as needed
- *Participative decision making.* Level of active exploration of a full range of choices; effort to create mutually supported alteratives or win-win decisions
- *Problem-solving and analytical skills.* Contribution to team problem solving; anticipation of potential problems; ability to develop alternatives and suggest best choices
- *Credibility and trust.* How openly the member expresses both facts and feelings
- *Work processes and procedures.* Adherence to standard work processes and procedures
- *Integration of technical skills.* Ability to learn new skills from other team members (e.g., financial data, computer systems)
- *Interdependence.* Level of recognition of the importance of others, including the organization as a whole; interest shown in involving others in the identification and solution of problems/issues
- *Managing skills.* Ability to demonstrate management skills, including budgeting, inventory, scheduling, and leadership
- *Commitment.* Level of commitment to the idea of work teams
- *Interpersonal relations.* How the member strives to maintain good relationships with teammates, managers, and other teams and support services
- *Initiation of ideas.* How frequently the member suggests ideas, alternatives, and solutions

- *Leadership.* How the member shares the leadership role; occasionally assumes responsibility for leading the team
- *Acceptance of change and risk taking:* How receptive the member is to change; willingness to change own behavior, explore new ideas, stimulate risk taking

For legal purposes, it's important to define the acceptable and unacceptable behaviors that fit each factor. Team members must be consistent about what constitutes good or poor behavior.

A secondary benefit to spending time as a team defining behaviors and building an evaluation tool is that all team members become very aware of the team's behavior/performance standards.

Sample Evaluation Processes

Probationary Evaluation for New Team Members

A team culture emphasizes the importance of ongoing communication. The most obvious example is the regular performance reviews for all new team members after six weeks, twelve weeks, and eighteen weeks (see Figure 6-1).

Sample Measures After Six-Week Period

- Satisfactory completion of specialized training (e.g., statistical process control, team building)
- Satisfactory completion of quality training
- Satisfactory completion of equipment training
- Dependability (reports to work daily and promptly; follows instructions and procedures)
- Teamwork (receptive to basic team concepts; contributes in team meetings)
- Communication (initiates communication with others, including team leader)

Sample Measures After Twelve-Week Period

- Productivity and efficiency (meets production goals; workflow is smooth)

Figure 6-1. Six-week probationary review form for team members.

____________________ __________
Name of Person Evaluated Job Title

____________________ __________
Name of Evaluator Date

Job Factor	Rating		Comments
	Needs Improvement	Satisfactory or Above	
Specialized Training Satisfactory completion of specialized training (e.g., SPC, team building).	☐	☐	
Quality Training Satisfactory completion of quality training.	☐	☐	
Equipment Training Satisfactory completion of equipment training.	☐	☐	
Dependability Reports to work daily and promptly; follows instructions and procedures.	☐	☐	
Teamwork Receptive to basic team concepts; contributes in team meetings.	☐	☐	
Communication Initiates communication with others, including team leader.	☐	☐	

- Process knowledge (understands own operations; able to explain basic operations to others)
- Special training (able to construct charts, collect data, calculate limits)
- Cross-training (can train others within area; takes initiative to learn operations outside immediate area)
- Dependability (reports promptly; follows procedures with some guidance)
- Teamwork (understands teamwork; is willing to work as part of the team)
- Communication (asks questions for clarification; opening communication within the team)

With the growing use of hiring teams to conduct applicant interviews and make hiring recommendations and decisions, the role of the hiring team during performance reviews is expanding. The hiring team can be used to provide feedback on the new hire's actual performance compared to original expectations.

Q&A #5, 11

Self-Directed Work Team Evaluation Process

A number of organizations have been using team evaluations for several years. Here is a sample structure and process that is commonly used:

1. The team meets with the team manager to set team objectives for a specified period of time.
2. Members receive training on performance planning and evaluating.
3. Team members discuss and establish individual performance objectives and standards and methods of measurement.
4. The team determines how performance will be reviewed and submits plan and process steps to the team manager or human resources manager for review and approval. Options include the following:
   - All team members evaluate each other, and results are tabulated.
   - Two members of the team, one picked by the person

being reviewed and one picked by the rest of the team, conduct and deliver the performance evaluation.
- A chairperson selected by the team member being evaluated assembles a group of three or four people to evaluate performance.

5. Members receive training on coaching skills and conducting performance reviews, as well as on how to receive and process feedback.
6. Throughout the project, the team participates in ongoing coaching and review. The team manager and supervisor and other teams provide regular feedback about the team's progress.
7. As the final review approaches, the team member completes a self-evaluation, and the entire team completes a written evaluation on the member. In addition, customer surveys and written evaluations from other independent teams may be added. All of the results are tabulated.
8. The two team members or any similar configuration (see item 4) review the information (self-evaluation plus others' evaluation), identify areas of congruence and incongruence, decide how closely objectives were achieved, and pinpoint areas for continued growth.
9. The evaluators meet with the team member and review the information, completing a final form that combines all the information. The evaluation includes the development of a performance plan including new goals and skills growth for the duration of the project.

Digital Equipment Corporation uses a team of five people as evaluators: a chairperson picked by the person being evaluated, a manager, two team members selected at random, and the individual being evaluated. Each role is defined and the process steps identified.[2]

Tips for the Team Review Interview

- Set a mutually agreeable time for review discussion after all material (self-evaluation, customer surveys, team member reviews) is received and compiled.

- Arrange for private space, and allow no interruptions.
- Warmly greet the team member.
- Explain how the interview process will proceed; ask for suggestions from the team member.
- Offer the team member the opportunity to choose where to begin.
- Ask open-ended questions (how, why) to encourage a two-way discussion.
- Use actual examples of the member's performance to explain reasons for the team's rating.
- In areas needing improvement, discuss behavior that can be changed and the specific improvements desired.
- Stress specific improvement goals, rather than focusing on past mistakes.
- Reach agreement on performance improvement goals.
- Summarize discussion points.
- Explain any next steps (such as the completion of the final form).
- Explain the appeal process if the evaluation is negative.
- Schedule follow-up coaching sessions to review the team member's progress.

Unacceptable Interview Behaviors

- Surprising the team member with an impromptu review
- Not reading through all the evaluations and compiling results into an understandable format
- "Winging it" during the interview
- Generalizing about behavior; providing no specific examples
- Asking the team member to change his/her personality, rather than behavior
- Taking phone calls and interruptions during the interview
- Dominating the discussion; being unwilling to listen to the team member's explanation
- Being unwilling to admit that the evaluators' assessment of a situation may have been wrong after hearing the team member's explanation

- Suggesting the team member is responsible for entire success or failure of the team
- Ending the interview without providing a summary and setting new performance goals
- Having no follow-up plan to review ongoing performance

Handling Problem Evaluation Situations

Q&A #2, 4

Teams are increasingly finding themselves in the situation of conducting or participating in probationary reviews that may result in discharge. Here are some critical issues for the team to consider:

- Does the team member qualify under a protected class (age, sex, race, national origin, handicap, and so on)?
- Was the team's request for a behavioral change on the part of the new worker reasonable and related to the safe and efficient performance of the job?
- Did the team member receive adequate warning of the consequences of misconduct?
- Did the team investigate the matter before administering discipline?
- Was the team's investigation objective?
- Did the team obtain substantial evidence that the member's behavior was a problem?
- Has the team, and any other team in the organization, applied its rules, orders, and penalties in a manner similar to that of all other teams?
- Did the team identify the desired change in behavior or performance and allow adequate time for the change to occur?
- Do the organization's written policies support the activities of the team?

Defamation of Character/Invasion of Privacy

Q&A #10

During a disciplinary or discharge proceeding, only those who have a legitimate interest in or who are integrally involved in the team member's performance evaluation and discharge decision should have knowledge of the proceedings. Those without legitimate interest should not be told confidential information.

We encourage teams to be specially trained in discipline and discharge procedures before proceeding because of the potential legal ramifications of the team's actions. Handling these issues is extremely difficult for a team, and yet we have seen teams handle them very effectively from both a task and a relationship viewpoint.

Team Reward Systems

More and more organizations are beginning to redesign their reward systems to reflect team values. Gainsharing and other group bonus systems are becoming more common, as are informal rewards that single out teams, rather than individuals.

Teams, just like individuals, respond to both external and internal rewards. Examples of external rewards include pay, bonuses, plaques, notes, publicity in newspapers, commendations at a company party, certificates, gifts, trips, and dinners. Examples of internal rewards include satisfaction from accomplishing the team goal and a sense of well-being deriving from strong work relationships, creative challenges, increased responsibility, and learning opportunities.

Special Tips on Team Reward Systems

- The reward system must be congruent with the culture in the organization and with the overall management style.
- If the evaluation system stresses one set of priorities and the reward system stresses another, the reward system will win out.
- People will work hardest on tasks for which they receive the greatest rewards (Vroom, 1964; Lawler, 1973).
- The reward system must focus on the accomplishments of the team, not individuals (Mower and Wilemon, 1989).
- Reward and recognition systems geared to individuals are in direct conflict with the idea of teams.

- If the organization is going to give rewards, it is best to do so at the end of a team project, rather than on an annual basis.
- Evaluations based on the amount of time members spend on a team may not provide the best measure of their contribution.
- If a team is not highly autonomous, providing rewards at the team level may be counterproductive (Lawler and Cohen, 1992).
- Reward systems should make teams accountable to the organization as a whole, as well as to the team.
- Pay-for-performance and job-based compensation systems do not fit the requirements of self-directed and self-managed work teams because they reward individual accomplishments more than team results (Lawler and Cohen, 1992).

Before deciding on a particular reward system, management and the team need to address the following critical questions:

- Who should be included in the reward system (e.g., original suggesters, implementation team)?
- Who should be the recognizer (management, team members)?
- How much money constitutes an effective reward?
- How much information should be shared about how rewards are determined and who gets them?
- How should rewards be handled when the members of the team change during a project?
- What rewards (informal and formal) would be considered meaningful by the team?
- How should rewards differ for different types of teams (cross-functional vs. self-directed, for example)?

Roles in the Reward System

The Role of Management

Q&A #15

- Spearheading a feasibility assessment that addresses the question, Does our current reward system value teams?

- Creating a collaborative process for defining desired changes in the reward system
- Analyzing current reward practices
- Educating teams about reward system alternatives
- Assisting with the design and development of a team reward system
- Scheduling and managing long-term team skill acquisition
- Monitoring results and evaluating any changes
- Gathering and recording supporting evidence for the team review
- Assisting with quantifying aspects of performance that are not easily measurable

Q&A #7

The Role of the Team

- Managing the performance evaluation system
- Identifying team accomplishments
- Evaluating team member performance
- Identifying new skills and providing skill certification
- Suggesting and recommending changes to the reward system
- Assisting in the distribution of rewards
- Providing feedback about the reward system to management

Simple Team Reward Systems

Sometimes the team process has been established before any formal reward system is in place. It's still important to recognize the accomplishments of a team. Here is a step-by-step process:

1. The team needs to develop criteria for recognition standards (e.g., what will be considered meaningful?). Remember to give as much weight to the team's use of process as to the results achieved.

   Q&A #8

   Recognition of a task well done:
   - Receiving a personal note, memo, or preprinted card
   - Being given a new, different task
   - Presenting results to upper-level group

- Hearing positive comments
- Having team results used by others in organization
- Receiving additional training
- Hearing accomplishments announced at a meeting

Recognition of important accomplishments (this is more formal and usually includes the supervisor):

- Having a note placed in personnel file
- Receiving a token gift or recognition at an annual event
- Enjoying greater range in next team assignment
- Having team serve as consultant for other teams

Recognition of outstanding and truly significant performance:

- Receiving a public reward
- Enjoying strong supervisory support for involvement
- Having a note placed in personnel file
- Being an honored guest at an awards event
- Having advice sought on new projects
- Receiving visits from top management
- Enjoying greater freedom and authority
- Having the opportunity to master new state-of-the-art skill

2. Management then solicits nominations from anyone in the organization.
3. Management selects teams whose accomplishments meet the criteria and will be seen as significant by all employees.
4. Management broadcasts team accomplishments in a company newsletter or on company bulletin boards.
5. Management uses a special event to honor winning teams.
6. Management presents achievement certificates and awards.

Complex Team Reward Systems

Dramatic shifts are occurring in the area of compensation as a result of the shift to a team culture. The traditional approach of rewarding individual accomplishment is in direct opposition to team concepts. Experts agree that gainsharing and skill-based pay are fast becoming the most widely used compensation programs for teams (see Figure 6-2).

Figure 6-2. Pay options for teams.

Types of Pay Options	*How the System Works*	*Benefits*	*Drawbacks*
Traditional job-based or pay-for-performance	Rewards individuals on basis of position, seniority, or individual merit.	Simple; a standard used by most organizations.	Rewards on an annual schedule. Focuses on individual achievement—not effective for teams. Does not encourage people to learn other skills.
Skill-based/knowledge-based	Rewards individuals for acquiring needed skills. Team members test and certify that new skill has been achieved.	Encourages acquiring of new team skills. Can attract and retain right skill mix.	Not effective for teams that meet only several hours per week. Cost-effective only when persons with needed skills cannot be hired easily.
Gainsharing	Returns a share of the cost savings above a specified and agreed-upon level to all employees.	Good for project and self-directed work teams. Increases employee knowledge of the "big picture finances." Participatory decision making.	Requires assistance with implementation and administration. Savings are shared among all, even though a single team may be responsible.
Team bonus	Team members share in a percentage of the estimated savings when important targets are met or at the end of a project.	Effective for project teams. Simple system that works best for teams that stand alone as performing units.	Estimated cost savings may not be realized. Members may feel that system is unfair because they receive only a percentage of the savings.
Collective pay-for-performance or merit-pay system	Evaluation is based on the effectiveness of a total unit and team performance appraisals.	Covers a total organizational unit, rather than individual teams. Good for project organizations seeking long-term relationships among teams.	Who should share may become an issue.

Questions and Answers: Overcoming Evaluation Difficulties

1. **Q.** *How do you handle people who say they have their "real" work and their team work?*

   A. People are smart enough to do the work that is rewarded. If an organization puts enough emphasis on customer, quality, and teamwork in the evaluation tool, it doesn't take employees long to change their emphasis. However, if the organization keeps the old evaluation tool, those job factors emphasized in that tool will continue to be the important ones.

2. **Q.** *How do you know when to discipline a team member?*

   A. The team needs to examine, first, whether the member has the competency to do the job. If not, then the team will need to provide training and/or skill development to bring the competency up to an acceptable level. However, if the competency is there and the team member is simply refusing (lacks the commitment) to do the task, then the team should decide on a disciplinary approach.

3. **Q.** *Why would someone refuse to do a task or show low commitment?*

   A. There are a number of reasons. First, sometimes good work is punished (team members may joke about someone who is prompt or who gets work done on time). Poor behavior is often negatively reinforced because everyone focuses a lot of attention on it (similar to a two-year-old's tantrum). Good behavior is sometimes ignored or, worse yet, rewarded by giving the hard worker additional assignments.

4. **Q.** *Should a team ever be responsible for discipline or discharge?*

   A. We have seen teams handle discipline and discharge very carefully and effectively with adequate training. One extremely important issue is privacy protection. It takes special effort when five or ten people are involved in a decision to keep the actions and decisions of the team confidential.

5. **Q.** *How do you set performance goals for a team member?*

   A. The goals can be based on business measures, such as reduction in cycle time, cost of operations, or rate of productivity, or they can reflect quality measures, such as meeting customer requirements or other specifications. Individual team member goals should be microcosms of the broader team goal.

   A goal should be specific, measurable, achievable, results-oriented, and time-bound. We have found that many team members have difficulty writing goals and often end up writing specific solutions, rather than goals. For example, rather than defining the goal ("improved communication between the design and production teams"), they might state a solution ("weekly meetings between design and production").

6. **Q.** *What about other types of evaluation tools?*

   A. There are many tools on the market for evaluating both a team's effectiveness and the skill of individual members. New computer software allows a person to be evaluated by others, with only the manager having access to all the feedback. Because so many organizations are using teams, the necessary tools and software will likely follow soon.

7. **Q.** *Do people ever say they don't get paid enough to take on what was traditionally management's headache?*

   A. Sure they do. Giving performance evaluations can be very stressful for people, particularly if any problems exist in performance. Add to that our basic dislike of conflict, and it's no wonder team members object.

   Part of accepting the role of evaluator is understanding how much people truly value feedback. A 1986 Bureau of National Affairs survey showed that employees feel that the most important communication they receive from management is information and feedback on job performance (rather than information about company benefits). Most people want to know how they're doing, whether their work has value. When an evaluator recognizes the gift he or she is giving the person in the form of honest and direct feedback, it changes the attitude toward the role.

8. **Q.** *Are there small rewards a team can be given if you don't have a whole reward system in place?*

   A. We encourage teams to keep success logs (see Figure 6-3) that record every time a goal is achieved or something is handled particularly well. If the team is aware of a cost savings they've achieved, it should note this on the log. The success log can be posted for all to see or given to top management on a regular basis.

   One team rings a bell hanging in the office every time it gets or completes a large contract. One note: People who grew up being told not to "blow their own horn" may need some time to get comfortable with this idea. However, the visual change in affect that occurs when a team celebrates its success is amazing: eyes light up, posture straightens, smiles abound.

9. **Q.** *Are you saying that the traditional pay systems don't work for teams?*

   A. Pay systems that reward seniority, a single narrow skill, or position by title have little value in a team environment. People repeat behavior that gets rewarded. If pay is based on a set of measurements that emphasize great customer service, great customer service will occur. Therefore, if an organization rewards the number of years someone has worked or the fact that someone holds a particular position, employees will focus more on these measures than on team building, collaboration, and facilitation.

   In most companies, changes in the compensation system lag behind the culture change to teams.

10. **Q.** *Can legal problems result if a team does a performance evaluation?*

Figure 6-3. Sample action items/success log.

Week of ___ / ___ / ___ /

ACTION ITEMS	*SUCCESSES*
(List here all the commitments made by team members to do specific tasks.)	*(List here all the successes the team can identify in a specific week.)*

A. Most of the legal problems arising from evaluations occur when the information on them is used in a discharge. For example, if an evaluator discriminates by inflating the ratings of one employee while deflating another's ratings or if an evaluation is used to retaliate against an employee who has filed a sexual harassment complaint, these issues will surface during any legal proceeding.

A team must be made aware of the legal significance of what is it doing and the potential impact of its actions on the company. Proper training is crucial here, including a clear understanding of the purpose of evaluations, the importance of fair and equitable ratings, skill in how to give performance feedback, and proper recordkeeping.

11. **Q.** *Are there any special risks for teams when doing peer evaluations?*

A. Teams, simply because they are groups, take more risks than do single individuals. Consequently, the natural hesitancy to make judgments is reduced and teams may evaluate more critically than would a single manager.

Sometimes people think that teams will be more lenient, but we have not found this to be the case. Empowered by each other, team members are much more demanding regarding one another's performance.

12. **Q.** *Do you suggest annual evaluations for teams?*

A. We don't suggest annual evaluations for anyone. Evaluations should be done quarterly or at least semiannually to be effective. For teams, evaluations should be done when certain milestones in a project are achieved or, in the case of self-directed work teams, on at least a semiannual basis.

13. **Q.** *What if we're having trouble getting the organization to change to meet the needs of the team?*

A. There are several options. The team can design a questionnaire asking members to respond to key questions about the evaluation/compensation system. Armed with data, the team can then meet with its manager. Perhaps several teams can do a survey and combine their results. Typically, such surveys show that people have great difficulty with a traditional evaluation system in a team culture because the wrong things are being measured by the wrong people.

14. **Q.** *If Deming of Total Quality Management fame is so opposed to evaluations, why not just eliminate them?*

    A. Good question. In most companies, evaluations are the most important pieces of paper in any discharge situation. When the courts ask, "Was this person aware that there was a performance problem?" it's the evaluation document that is most often used as evidence.

    Too many managers would not give any feedback to employees if they weren't forced to. It's not just a problem with negative evaluations, either. For some managers, praising an employee is as difficult as criticizing.

15. **Q.** *Are there special tips for a team handling its own compensation decisions for the first time?*

    A. We recently worked with a self-directed work team handling its own compensation decisions for the first time. The owner of the company assisted the team by distributing in advance a memo with his philosophy and views on compensation. He asked team members to complete a confidential questionnaire to gather their opinions on privacy, distribution formulas, skill-based pay, and key behaviors that team members were to observe during any discussions on compensation. This owner was particularly aware of the sensitive nature of compensation. By giving members an opportunity to voice their concerns in advance, he was able to prepare for any "smoking guns" and to address team member concerns as the team took on this new responsibility.

Notes

1. R. Aguayo, *Dr. Deming, The American Who Taught the Japanese About Quality* (New York: Carol, 1990).
2. C. A. Norman and R. A. Zawacki, "Team Appraisals—Team Approach," *Personnel Journal* 70, no. 9 (September 1991): 101–104.

Chapter 7
Training

As organizations develop and design their team training programs, they need to make sure that certain critical ingredients are present.

Characteristics of Effective Training

- Provides an opportunity to share life experiences with other adults
- Allows some control and self-direction in the learning process
- Establishes a correlation between prior experience and new skill development
- Encourages active participation and provides the opportunity to do the tasks
- Has warm, friendly atmosphere receptive to the contributions of those attending
- Provides for practical application of new material
- Includes numerous repetitions of the same information in different formats
- Provides frequent, specific, and accurate feedback
- Offers an opportunity to ask questions

Adult Learning

Most adults are not receptive to sitting for long periods of time to hear lectures or to participating in activities that require lots of risk taking (e.g., some role plays) and that invite negative criticism given in front of peers. Instead, they prefer:

- Being asked what their concerns are
- Being told what will occur
- Being given an opportunity to explain what they already know about a topic
- Receiving an effective demonstration and explanation
- Hearing about real-life stories and examples
- Being given a chance to practice
- Having a specific follow-up plan

The design of a training program includes both the gathering of information and the processing of information. These two steps utilize a number of different instructional methods.

1. *Gathering information.* The two methods of gathering information are active and passive. The active methods use direct involvement through group discussion, simulations and role plays, programmed instruction, games, and case studies. The passive methods stress absorption through lectures and presentations, readings, panels, and demonstrations.

2. *Processing information.* The two methods of processing information are deductive (from general to specific) and inductive (from specific to general). Again, deductive methods include lectures and presentations, group discussion, readings, panels, and case studies in which participants have to make their own application. Inductive methods include role plays and simulations, programmed instruction, games, and demonstrations in which participants take a specific situation and apply it to all.

A well-designed training program recognizes the two methods of gathering and the two methods of processing information and incorporates as many variations as possible in the design.

Team Training

To be successful team members, employees must receive substantial and periodic training spread over time that addresses two distinct needs: how to function as a team in terms of structures and tasks and how to relate to people as team players. All too often, organizations spend considerable training dollars developing the task skills (how to set up and run meetings) and pay little attention to the relationship skills that fundamentally make or break a team.

The goal of all team training is to improve the awareness, understanding, knowledge, and skill of team members in six transformational areas:

1. Coping with change
2. Accepting responsibility
3. Functioning as a team
4. Achieving personal and team growth
5. Engaging in critical thinking
6. Working on continuous personal improvement

Curriculum Development

Organizations that have in-house training capability may find it possible to mix and match various existing communication and conflict resolution programs with team building training. Curriculum content should be carefully checked to avoid overlap with existing programs. Scripted training modules may be purchased to help integrate the task and relationship learning sequences that are necessary for the team's development.

Organizations that do not have in-house trainers may want to consider contracting with an experienced independent trainer to provide the training. Most professional trainers can modify module content to meet the needs of an organization and work carefully to move the team from a dependent state to an independent state. Canned presentations and videotape series that do not allow for interaction and flexibility in design are not appropriate for team building.

The content of each training module is typically determined by the trainer on the basis of input about the skills team members want or need to learn. It is also helpful to discuss with the team the purpose behind various exercises, particularly when the purpose is not readily apparent. In one case, the sixteen men on a self-directed work team in a shipping department objected strongly to any team exercises in which they had to share feelings or experiences that were not work-related. Only as the team's responsibilities became more clear did the men begin to acknowledge the value of improving their interpersonal skills. Luckily, the plant manager was not easily swayed to the men's early negative evaluations of the training.

Training modules for teaching transformational skills need to include the following:

For Task Development: Administrative Skills

Group 1: Defining the elements of effective teams
Defining types of teams
Understanding the roles team members play
Holding effective meetings
Reaching team consensus

Group 2: Becoming an effective facilitator
Problem solving as a team
Understanding the changing role of the supervisor
Strategic planning and goal setting in teams
Developing critical thinking skills

Group 3: Evaluating and rewarding team performance
Launching self-directed or self-managed work teams
Giving winning presentations

For Interpersonal Development

Group 1: Understanding human behavior
Defining team behaviors
Appreciating differences in style and personality
Communicating trust and credibility
Developing quality customer service

Group 2: Handling difficult people
Resolving conflicts as a team
Problem solving in relationships
Receiving feedback and deciding what to do about it

Group 3: Building strong team relationships with MBTI (Myers-Briggs Type Indicator)
Managing and sustaining the change dynamic
Setting standards: team ethics
Managing diversity of thought and background
Influencing without authority

Supervisory Training

Most people are promoted to the supervisory level on the basis of their ability to do specific tasks, not because of their ability to coach and influence others. A very different set of skills is required in order for a supervisor to work successfully with a team. In addition to regular team training, supervisors generally benefit from additional training in these areas:

- Comprehending the changing role of the supervisor
- Listening to and encouraging others' opinions
- Providing team meeting support (when to help, when to step aside)
- Guiding and facilitating win-win conflict resolution
- Creating the components of a trusting, respectful environment
- Appreciating diversity in the work force
- Learning to manage and discipline one's own behavior
- Empowering others—zapping versus sapping energy
- Effective delegating and "hand-off" plans
- Collaborating: Two heads are better than one
- Teaching others to solve their own problems

We have found it particularly valuable to spend at least ten to twelve hours with supervisors and managers in advance of any team launch. This intensive period of skill development helps them appreciate the effort that will be required of hourly staff while simultaneously alleviating some of the pride and self-esteem issues that arise when supervisors and hourly staff are first blended as a team.

One team complained after two training sessions that everything was going too slowly and said it was ready to start. The manager, who had already been working with members for four weeks, was able to recognize that their assessment was not valid and, by using work examples to show the importance of building the team slowly, helped convince the team to slow down.

Needs Assessment

Any effective training program begins with a needs assessment that answers a number of questions, including the following:

- What training has been given so far? To whom? How long ago?
- How did people respond to the previous training?
- What do organization decision-makers see as the primary needs to be met by this training? Why?
- What level of resistance exists toward training? Why (e.g., previous training was never used on the job)?
- What is the existing structure in the organization? Will team building complement or contradict existing structure?
- How will training be used? How will training be regularly reinforced?

Training is not a gift or a punishment. Training is an investment that the organization makes in its own future.

Pretraining Assessment

People come to the team building process with a wide range of skills and abilities. It is often wise to have individuals complete a pretraining assessment to determine the skill level of each member. A pretraining assessment also provides the organization with starting-point data against which to measure the success of the training.

Key Points About Assessing Skills

- Assessments make some people very anxious and may not be worth the anxiety that they produce.

- The assessment should be presented as a tool to be used to design and provide effective training, not as a device to be used for punitive or judgmental purposes.
- The tool itself must have validity as an appropriate testing instrument.
- The results must be shared with the individual, with goals set for key areas needing improvement.
- Individual results should be confidential, although a team composite may be shared.

The Role of the Trainer

Trainers are facilitators, not star performers. If the trainer focuses on meeting his or her own needs, then the trainer is playing the star. A good trainer focuses on the participants' needs. Are the participants comfortable? Are they learning? Are they actively involved? What can be done to improve the learning environment?

Trainers should foster independence, not dependence. There is no point in making participants dependent on a trainer unless a trainer expects to always be there—a virtual impossibility. In team training, a trainer must share center stage with participants and fundamentally believe there is a wealth of knowledge present in each person in the room.

Not everyone can be an effective trainer. Certain characteristics are critically important in trainers.

Qualities of Effective Trainers

- Willingness to train
- Willingness to practice, prepare, and work hard at doing a good job
- A patient and friendly demeanor
- Good communication skills, including clear speech, confident presence, and approachable manner
- Ability to use humor wisely and well
- Ability to earn respect
- Ability to engage others in the process
- Flexibility and open-mindedness

- General air of amiability; lack of pretentiousness or pomposity

Training Session Structure and Tips

Every training program should begin by introducing both the participants and the trainers, stating the training objectives (what will be learned), and announcing housekeeping details (where bathrooms are located, time and length of breaks, and so on).

Breaks

Typically, breaks should occur about every one and a half hours to allow participants to move around, rejuvenate, and allow previous training to sink in. When the break occurs, tell participants when they are expected to return.

Q&A #7

Cotraining

Cotraining is exciting and tricky. Cotrainers need to work out ahead of time exactly who will do each piece of the training. If cotrainers intend to ask each other to give opinions or ideas, they should plan when that will occur ahead of time. When one trainer is training, the cotrainer should occupy a seat off to one side. During group work, both trainers should move among the groups. Some trainers develop a signal to alert each other if they are having trouble and need help (a marker or pen placed in an unnatural position could be an alert signal). Most important, both trainers need to respect each other's space and style and avoid throwing curves or competing during the training session.

Flip Charts

Flip-chart sheets can be prepared either in advance or as the session evolves. New trainers sometimes find that it helps them keep on track if they prepare in advance. One trick is to write on the flip chart in light pencil the key points to be made so that participants don't realize that "crib notes" are being used.

Always work to one side or the other of the flip chart. Use dark markers only (black, blue, red, or green). Printing should be about two-inches high to ensure readability.

Group Work

There are rules you can follow to help you work with groups of varying sizes.

1. *Large groups.* The key here is to ask a question and then allow sufficient time for someone to respond. If a trainer jumps in too quickly with the answer, a pattern is established and the group will not respond. If a trainer has problems getting responses, choose a strong member (this is guesswork), and ask for his/her response.

2. *Group within a group.* The trainer selects five to seven people to serve as a primary group (in the center), and the remaining participants function as observers by forming a circle around the primary group. Both the primary group and the observers may report out on the group's effort.

3. *Small groups.* Divide the people into small groups the first time by counting off (e.g., all ones together, all twos together, and so on). Groups should not exceed five people. Encourage participants to move their chairs around so that all group members can hear each other and participate. This is vitally important to the group process. The trainer should plan to move around and listen to each of the groups to assess whether they are functioning well. If the trainer senses that participants are uncomfortable with his or her presence, the trainer can ask the group if it's okay to listen in on their discussion.

   If the groups are not functioning well or have established cliques, have participants count off (one to five) for the next group activity and form new groups. It's an easy way to reformat groups without having to discuss their earlier problems.

4. *Three-person groups.* Here two people function as partners, and the third person acts as an observer. After the exercise, the observer gives feedback to the other two about what he or she saw and heard.

5. *Partners.* Two-person groups can be formed either by the trainer or by just telling people to find a partner. It's possible that a person will not have a partner; in that case, the trainer will have to function as a partner.

Overhead Transparencies

Overhead transparencies should be large enough for all participants to see. The trainer should work from the overhead machine and not the screen or wall. The trainer should face the audience and point via the transparency on the machine. Do not turn your back on the participants.

Positioning

It's important to take a strong position at the beginning of training (front and center, head up and back straight). Cotrainers should position left and right of center. Practice assuming the beginning position many times before the actual day. Avoid mirror positions (hands in pockets or on hips, feet at same position). Eyes should always be making contact with participants and scanning both sides of the room. Everyone has a dominant side; it's important to practice scanning toward the weaker side. Move around to both sides, but do not pace or rock from side to side. Hand gestures should emphasize what is being said. Open palms encourage participation. Do not hold things (paper clips, rubber bands, or your workbook) in your hands for long periods, for we all have a tendency to fiddle with things when we are nervous. Never hold a single piece of paper or anything that will move if nervousness is a problem.

Questions From Participants

Encourage questions from participants by responding in a manner that suggests their question is important. If a trainer needs "think" time, ask the person to restate the question so you can understand it better or ask the person to give you an example of what he or she means. As the person does that, you will actually be working on your response.

If you do not have an answer, say so, and ask if any of the participants might have encountered a similar situation and can provide a response. Sometimes, it's wise to do this even when the trainer has an answer but feels the group is becoming too dependent on his or her leadership.

Resistance

Q&A #9

If you have a difficult participant (and usually there is one in every group), plan to go with the resistance (i.e., "I see what you mean. Boy, that is a difficult problem."). Then ask the larger group if anyone sees it differently. At all costs, avoid a "them-versus-me" situation.

If participants are chit-chatting during the training, the best answer is to approach the pair during a break and tell them that you have a problem with their talking and ask them to stop. Don't take them on during active training, but don't let it go unresolved, either.

If the trainer encounters strong group resistance, stop the training and ask the group to talk about what is wrong. Often something else is troubling them (an announcement in the organization or an interpersonal feud) and keeping them from concentrating on the training. Allow them to vent and use the problem as a hands-on, problem-solving exercise by refocusing from the problem to their goal and discussing how they can go about achieving it.

It's important not to allow a training session to disintegrate into a gripe session. Put time boundaries on the discussion and create an "Unresolved Issues" flip-chart sheet so training can continue.

Role Plays

Do not attempt role plays until participants feel relaxed and open with each other. Also, remember that some people have great difficulty with role play. If someone resists, suggest that the person observe for a while or function as the "difficult one" in the role play, rather than the person who is trying to do it right.

Follow these rules of thumb with role plays:

- Describe the role play as a laboratory setting where people can experiment with new behavior.
- State that one of the rules is that the person experimenting can call "time out" any time he or she wishes to start over.
- Note that you will ask the participants in the role play to speak first (after the role play) and identify what they particularly liked about what they did and what they would want to change for next time.
- Allow the viewers to give their opinions after the participants have spoken. Do not allow people to attack the role players.
- At the end of each role play and discussion, give the participants a round of applause for their effort.

Items to Have on Hand for Training

- Adequate number of markers
- Praise stickers
- 3- by 5-inch index cards (for name cards or written exercises)
- Training certificates (last day)
- Masking tape
- Flip charts and easel
- Extra pens or pencils
- Blank transparencies
- Overhead projector
- Extra overhead projector light bulb
- Cough drops
- Evaluations
- Extra workbooks
- Training videotape, VCR, TV
- Video camera/blank videotapes

Q&A #3, 6

Using Nonprofessional In-House Trainers

After people have participated in the initial training, they often develop an interest in being part of a team of nonprofessional in-house trainers.

In-house training is especially effective for (a) mid-size organizations that cannot afford outside professional training for all levels of employees and that do not have an in-house training staff, and (b) people who enjoy being trained by their peers who can relate to their needs and concerns.

In-house trainers need to complete training in the following areas before conducting any actual team training:

- Adult learning theory
- Training design and content
- Presentation skills (speech, delivery, personal presence, confidence and competence; use of training methods, tools, and equipment)
- How to handle specific difficult situations

Indications of Problems With In-House Training

When any of the following occur, it is important to stop and evaluate the effectiveness of in-house training.

- In-house trainer doesn't show up.
- Trainer fails to provide a clear statement of what is to be learned.
- There are numerous interruptions during training session.
- Supplies and equipment are lacking.
- The method of training is not consistent with written materials, training objectives, or adults learning theory.
- There are reports that training is disorganized.
- The trainers exhibit a poor attitude.
- There is a lack of written support materials.
- There are reports that questions are handled improperly.
- Trainers fail to make eye contact or to interact with participants.

Using Consultants and Outside Professional Trainers

People who function in teams are knee-deep in human relations. Often they experience trouble when given fluff training that focuses on superficial understanding and provides for little skill development. It is important to hire trainers and consultants who meet the needs of the team.

Q&A #10

Criteria for Hiring Outside Trainers

Encourage the development of a set of criteria that must be met by all outside contract trainers who wish to train your staff. If the trainers are unfamiliar with your organization's work, require them to provide the following:

- A five- to ten-minute video they developed for another similar training program
- References
- A preview of workshop content, outline, and workbook
- Evaluations by participants in a previous training program

Training an Entire Organization

Training an entire organization in team building skills presents numerous challenges. Here are four ideas to consider:

1. Set up a cross-functional training team to organize, schedule, and evaluate training modules.

2. Set up a training curriculum modeled after any typical college course listing, and offer each module at different times and on different dates. Some modules may be required prerequisites for more advanced training; if so, this should be noted on any sign-up sheet.

3. Contract with an outside trainer to design content and to train and prepare in-house trainers. The outside trainer serves as a coach and expert, while the in-house trainers do the actual delivery of material. The outside trainer also is responsible for maintaining quality and consistency among all the training sessions.

We have found that employees really enjoy learning from each other, particularly when the in-house trainers are well-prepared. It also demonstrates how people can learn to do new tasks and become quite good at them. For some employees, being an in-house trainer has provided new career opportunities and growth that have been exceedingly rewarding.

4. Establish a mentoring system in which an experienced employee coaches a newly trained person in team skills, discusses training content, and provides on-the-job feedback as the employee experiments with new behavior.

Evaluating and Testing Results

Q&A #11

Every training session should be evaluated on a number of key points:

- Was the program accurately described in any promotional material?
- Did the training session meet expectations?
- In what ways did it not meet expectations?
- Were you satisfied with the training content?
- What new skills were learned or improved upon?
- How will the skills learned in the program help you do a better job and contribute more to your work team?
- If you had designed the program, what would have been left the same? What would have been changed? What would have been added or deleted?
- How would you rate the instructors?
- Were the instructors prepared and organized?
- Did the instructors present information and use materials effectively?
- Did the instructors answer questions and encourage participation?

This list is presented in the form of a chart in Figure 7-1.

Follow-Up Testing

If participants completed a pretraining assessment, a posttraining assessment should be given within two weeks of the training. In

Figure 7-1. Training evaluation form.

We (I) would appreciate it if you would give us (me) your honest impression of this training program.

1. Was the program accurately described in written material?
   Yes ☐ No ☐
2. Did it meet your expectations? Yes ☐ No ☐
3. If you answered no to question 2, in what ways did it not meet your expectations? ______________________
   ____
4. Were you satisfied with the training content? Yes ☐ No ☐
5. What new skills were learned or improved upon? ______________________
   ____
6. How will the skills learned in the program help you do a better job/contribute more to your work team? ______________________
   ____
7. If you had designed the program, what would have been left the same? What would have been changed? What would have been added or deleted? ______________________
   ____
8. How would you rate the instructor(s)? ______________________
   ____
9. Was the instructor prepared and organized? Yes ☐ No ☐
10. Did the instructor present information and use materials effectively? Yes ☐ No ☐
11. Did the instructor answer questions and encourage participation?
    Yes ☐ No ☐

____
Name of Participant

addition, people often benefit from having follow-up assignments, maintaining training journals, and completing a three-month posttraining test.

Training Transfer

Ultimately, team building training will impact every facet of a person's life, both on and off the job. But initially, it may be hard to see immediate results. There may be a considerable time lag between developing an awareness in training and exhibiting new behavior on the job. Typical early results from training include friendlier interactions with coworkers, greater willingness to pitch in and help, and increased sensitivity to teams in other environments. Obviously, the more the training is applied on the job and supported by management and supervisors through discussion and practical application, the faster the transfer will occur.

Questions and Answers: Getting the Most Value From Training

1. **Q.** *Isn't outdoor training, such as wilderness or ropes training, the best method of teaching team building?*

   A. Approximately $45.5 billion is spent annually by corporate America on training and development, according to a report by *Training* magazine.[1] Only half of one percent of that (approximately $227 million) is spent on experienced-based (including outdoor) training.

   While outdoor training has many proponents who think it helps build trust and communication, competitive spirit, drive, and competence, many people have difficulty participating in this type of training. Typically, they cite the following reasons for their difficulty:

   - They find it hard to see the relevance and application of outdoor training to the in-office or production line setting.
   - The training places strenuous demands on physical capability and appeals most to outdoor types, rather than those with physical limitations.

- The training is expensive (most programs last four to ten days).
- There is a lack of follow-through back home.
- The training may cause conflicts with personal or religious beliefs.

However, others see benefits: a different environment in which to work through long-standing work conflicts or personality differences, a process of bringing everyone to a common denominator, improved mental attitude, and a way to allow people to see themselves as they really are under pressure, to name a few.

2. **Q.** *Isn't it difficult to teach the "soft skills" to people—don't they either have the ability to work with others or not?*

   A. For many, learning team building skills is like learning a foreign language. It's difficult at first, and everything has to be practiced over and over. The trainee may perform a behavior that he or she knows is wrong and pleadingly say, "Don't tell (the trainer) that I acted like that, okay?" Much of the final success will depend on how much the person wants to learn. If the desire is there, then anything is possible.

3. **Q.** *Is the quality of training lower with nonprofessional in-house trainers?*

   A. It doesn't have to be. If a trainer learns the material, does considerable outside reading on the topic, and carefully prepares examples and stories, there is no reason why he or she can't perform extremely well. However, if the training is approached as an afterthought with little or no preparation (especially for repeat trainings), then the quality will suffer. It's important for the organization to set quality standards for its training program and to measure quality continually to be certain those standards are met.

4. **Q.** *Some organizations have a professionally staffed in-house training department. Is it better to use this staff or to use contracted trainers from the outside?*

A. We suggest a blend of both. Use your in-house professional staff to train in areas where knowledge of the organization and its particular culture are important to the training module. A contract trainer is helpful when you want to see new approaches or techniques or when you need some people to be told that their behavior needs work. Often we are called in to play "hardball" with managers or supervisors who refuse to listen and learn. The outsider is often given more credence than the insider and can be more blunt (e.g., "No, voting is not a preferred option for teams") than an in-house trainer, who must be more careful to avoid stepping on toes.

5. **Q.** *What's the biggest mistake a trainer can make?*

A. Resting on past glories, rather than carefully preparing a master for each module every time. Even with lots of experience, it's difficult for a trainer to think of stories and examples during a training session—and often good stories are remembered long after the didactic (lecture) materials are forgotten.

6. **Q.** *How many in-house trainers should an organization have?*

A. It's reasonable to have between ten and fifteen in-house trainers, particularly if they are to cotrain. Different trainers can train on different topics, which creates nice variety for participants.

7. **Q.** *How does cotraining work?*

A. Two people present the material together, often rotating the presentation. Cotraining works especially well when both trainers can be involved at the same time. It's important to stress that any competitiveness between cotrainers is inappropriate and must be stopped immediately. Participants will feel the tension and will not learn as effectively as a result.

8. **Q.** *Sometimes people won't surface in training what is really troubling the team. What can you do about that?*

A. A good training session on trust or feelings can get the ball rolling, particularly if a question is asked that gets people talking (e.g., What causes trust to break down in teams?). If a participant knows there is a hidden agenda that should be surfaced, the person should be encouraged to talk with the trainer during a break. An experienced trainer will have numerous techniques to help a team discuss its problems.

In a group setting, it is important to set up the ground rules of discussion in advance so that the participants feel safe. We have found that most people won't open up with an inexperienced trainer who they feel may lose control of the situation.

9. **Q.** *What do you do with a problem participant who wants to pick holes in all the team building training?*

A. Some people find training to be a good opportunity to vent their feelings about a corporate decision. Often these occasions can provide great role-play situations. For example, the trainer can ask the group how long it wants to spend on the particular topic, how it wants to handle the discussion, and who wants to facilitate, process observe, and so on.

Most important, the trainer should never "position" opposite the participant by saying such things as, "You should do this or that." It's better to say, "What recommendations does the group have for how this situation might be handled?" Let the group respond, then the trainer can add a suggestion or two.

10. **Q.** *Is it good to use different training organizations to teach the team building?*

A. There's no problem with that, as long as the materials are coordinated and compatible. For example, one training company may use the terms "coordinator" or "facilitator" differently than another. It's especially important to have agreement on language.

We do believe that building a relationship with suppliers of training is an important part of the larger quality team concept. We encourage organizations to select one or two suppliers who then may subcontract other trainers but who assume quality control for those trainers brought in under the supplier's name.

11. **Q.** *Don't people object to testing in a team building environment?*

    A. That's a misconception. Teams can have very rigorous testing requirements and high standards and still keep a humanistic attitude. Probably sports teams are the best analogy here. Most teams do not tolerate mediocrity for the sake of harmony. They expect excellence in performance in both task and relationship activities.

12. **Q.** *Are there any pitfalls to avoid when training for team building?*

    A. It's important not to assume that participants understand and can apply the material simply because they've been taught it. The training needs to include time to practice what has been learned. Training labs are particularly effective because participants can do some "hands-on" work with the material. We find there is tremendous difference between a participant's ability to understand the new material and the ability actually to perform it. For example, a participant may be able to identify how to talk with a team member about a conflict, but, when asked to role play the discussion, the participant will often stumble over word choices, manner, or approach. To the inexperienced eye, it will look like none of the training has sunk in.

13. **Q.** *We've spent loads of money on team building training, and nothing has changed. What's wrong?*

    A. Don't assume that anything is wrong. We would be curious to hear the team's opinion of its progress. Often a manager or organizational leader judges a team's progress from a distance without having any real data to back up the opinion. It's unfair and demoralizing for the team.

    Sometimes progress is slow when the organization continues to reward (via compensation and promotion) behaviors that are not compatible with team building. It would be important to check the performance evaluation tools and compensation policies and procedures and make sure they are compatible.

Note

1. J. J. Laabs, "Team Training Goes Outdoors," *Personnel Journal* 70, no. 6 (June 1991): 56–63.

Bibliography

Aguren, S. *Volvo-Kalmar Revisited.* Gottenberg, Sweden: Development Council SAF LO PTC, 1985.

Aquilan, N. J. "Multiskilled Work Teams: Productivity Benefits." *California Management Review* 19 (1977): 17–22.

Argyris, C. *Integrating the Individual and the Organization.* New York: Wiley, 1964.

———. *Management and Organizational Development.* New York: McGraw-Hill, 1971.

Aubrey, C. A., and Felkins, P. K. *Teamwork: Involving People in Quality and Productivity Improvement.* White Plains, N.Y.: Quality Resources, 1988.

Baker, H. K. "The Hows and Whys of Team-Building." *Personnel Journal* 58 (June 1979): 367–370.

Bardwick, J. M. *Danger in the Comfort Zone.* New York: AMACOM, 1991.

Belbin, R. M. *Management Teams: Why They Succeed or Fail.* New York: Wiley, 1981.

Benson, T. E. "A Braver New World." *Industry Week* (August 3, 1992).

Berne, E. M. D. *The Structure and Dynamics of Organizations and Groups.* New York: Ballantine, 1963.

Blake, R. R., and Moulton, J. S. *The New Managerial Grid.* Houston, Tex.: Gulf, 1978.

———. "Overcoming Group Welfare." *Harvard Business Review* (November–December 1984): 98–108.

Boss, R. W. "The Effects of Leader Absence on a Confrontation Team-Building Design." *Journal of Applied Behavioral Science* 14 (1978): 469.

———. "It Doesn't Matter If You Win or Lose, Unless You're Losing: Organization Change in a Law Enforcement Agency." *Journal of Applied Behavioral Science* 15 (1979): 198.

Bradford, L. P., ed. *Group Development.* 2d ed. San Diego: University Associates, 1978.

Briggs, K. C., and Myers, I. B. "Myers-Briggs Type Indicator Assessment Form." Princeton, N.J.: Educational Testing Service, 1957.

Buchholz, S., and Roth, T. *Creating the High-Performance Team.* New York: Wiley, 1987.

Chance, P. "Great Experiments in Team Chemistry." *Across the Board* (May 1989): 18–24.

Cole, D. W. *Conflict Resolution Technology.* Cleveland, Ohio: Organization Development Institute, 1983.

Cummings, T. G. "Self-Regulating Work Groups: A Socio-Technical Synthesis." *Academy of Management Review* 3 (1978): 625–633.

Dailey, R. C. "The Effects of Cohesiveness and Collaboration on Work Groups: A Theoretical Model." *Group and Organizational Skills* 2 (1977): 461–469.

DeBono, E. *New Think.* New York: Avon, 1967.

Demeuse, K. P., and Liebowitz, S. J. "An Empirical Analysis of Team-Building Research." *Group and Organizational Skills* 6 (1981): 357–378.

Deming, W. E. *Out of the Crisis.* Cambridge, Mass.: Center for Advanced Engineering Study, 1988.

Drucker, P. F. "The Coming of the New Organization." *Harvard Business Review* 66 (1988): 45–53.

Dumaine, B. "What the Leaders of Tomorrow See." *Fortune* 120, no. 1 (1989): 48–62.

———. "Who Needs a Boss?" *Fortune* (1990): 52–55, 58, 60.

Dyer, W. G. *Team Building: Issues and Alternatives.* Reading, Mass.: Addison-Wesley, 1987.

Elden, M. "Socio-Technical Systems Ideas as Public Policy in Norway: Empowering Participation Through Worker Managed Change." *Journal of Applied Behavioral Science* 22 (1986): 239–255.

"Employee Involvement: Beyond Gamesmanship." *Industrial Relations News* (June 1981).

Ends, E. J., and Page, C. W. *Organizational Team Building.* Lanham, Md.: University Press of America, 1984.

Feder, R., and Mitchell, J. "4-Day Task Force More Efficient Than Traditional Problem-Solving." *Marketing News* (August 29, 1988): 21.

Francis, D., and Young, D. *Improving Work Groups: A Practical Manual for Team Building.* San Diego, Calif.: University Associates, 1979.

Glaser, E. M. "Productivity Gains Through Worklife Improvement." *Personnel* (January–February 1980): 70–78.

Glaser, R. *Facilitating Adult Learning in Semiautonomous Work Groups.* Ph.D. dissertation, Columbia University, 1991.

———. *How Independent Is Your Team?* King of Prussia, Pa.: Organization Design and Development, 1991.

———. *Moving Your Team Toward Self-Management.* King of Prussia, Pa.: Organization Design and Development, 1990.

———. *Self-Managing Teams: Learning to Be a Self-Managing Team.* King of Prussia, Pa.: Organization Design and Development, 1991.

Glaser, R., and Glaser C. *Building a Winning Management Team.* Bryn Mawr, Pa.: Organization Design and Development, 1986.

Golding, W. *Lord of the Flies.* New York: Putnam, 1954.

Goldstein, L. D. "Managers, Values, and OD." *Group and Organizational Skills* 18 (1983): 203–220.

Goodman, P. S. *Designing Effective Workgroups.* San Francisco: Jossey-Bass, 1986.

Guetzkow, H., and Dill, W. R. "Factors in the Organizational Development of Task Oriented Groups." *Sociometry* 20 (1957): 175.

Gulowsen, J. "A Measure of Work-Group Autonomy." In L. E. Davis and J. D. Taylor, eds., *Design of Jobs.* 2d ed. Santa Monica, Calif.: Goodyear, 1979.

Gwynne, S. C. "The Right Stuff." *Time* (October 29, 1990): 74–84.

Hackman, J. R. "The Psychology of Self-Management in Organizations." In M. S. Pollack and R. O. Perloff, eds., *Psychology and Work: Productivity Change and Employment* (89–136). Washington, D.C.: American Psychological Association, 1986.

Hackman, J. R., and Oldham, G. R. *Work Redesign.* Reading, Mass.: Addison-Wesley, 1980.

Harper, R., and Harper, A. *Succeeding as a Self-Directed Work Team.* Croton-on-Hudson, N.Y.: MW, 1989.

Haynes, M. E. *Effective Meeting Skills: A Practical Guide for More Productive Meetings.* Los Altos, Calif.: Crisp, 1988.

Herman, S. M., and Herman, M. O. "Special Teams, Properly Used, Can Create Effective Solutions." *Personnel Administrator* (October 1989): 90–92.

Hersey, P., and Blanchard, K. H. *Management of Organizational Behavior.* 5th ed. New York: Prentice Hall, 1988.

Hess, K., ed. *Creating the High Performance Team.* New York: Wiley, 1987.

Hoerr, J. "Getting Man and Machine to Live Happily Ever After." *Business Week* (April 20, 1987): 61–62.

———. "The Cultural Revolution at A. O. Smith." *Business Week* (May 29, 1989): 66–68.

———. "The Payoff From Teamwork." *Business Week* (July 10, 1989): 56–62.

———. "Work Teams Can Rev Up Paper Pushers, Too." *Business Week* (November 28, 1988): 68–69.

Hoerr, J., and Pollock, M. A. "Management Discovers the Human Side of Automation." *Business Week* (September 29, 1986): 74–77.

Houston, P. "Timberr." *Business Month* (December 1989): 50–56.

Hughes, B. "25 Stepping Stones for Self-Directed Work Teams." *Training* (December 1991): 44–46.

Hunsaker, P. L., and Curtis, W. *Managing Organizational Behavior*. Reading, Mass.: Addison-Wesley, 1986.

Huseman, R., and Hatfield, J. *Managing the Equity Factor*. Boston: Houghton Mifflin, 1989.

Jewell, L. N., and Reitz, H. J. *Group Effectiveness in Organizations*. Glenview, Ill.: Scott, Foresman, 1981.

Johnson, J. A. *Group Therapy: A Practical Approach*. New York: McGraw-Hill, 1963.

Kerr, S., Hill, K. D., and Broedling, L. "The First-Line Supervisor: Phasing Out or Here to Stay." *Academy of Management Review* 11 (1986): 103–117.

Ketchem, L. D. "How Redesigned Plants Really Work." *National Productivity Review* 3 (1984): 246–254.

Kiesler, S. B. *Interpersonal Processes in Groups and Organizations*. Arlington Heights, Ill.: AHM, 1978.

Klein, A. F. *Effective Groupwork*. Chicago: Association Press, 1972.

Klein, J. A. "Why Supervisors Resist Employee Involvement." *Harvard Business Review* (September–October 1984): 87–95.

Knowles, M. S. *The Adult Learner: A Neglected Species*. Houston, Tex.: Gulf, 1984.

Koprowski, E. J. "Improving Organization Effectiveness Through Action Research Teams." *Training and Development Journal* 26 (1972): 26–40.

Laabs, J. J. "Team Training Goes Outdoors." *Personnel Journal* 70, no. 6 (June 1991): 56–63.

Larson, C. E., and LaFasto, F. M. J. *Teamwork: What Must Go Right/What Can Go Wrong*. Newbury Park, Calif.: Sage, 1989.

Lawler, E. E. *High Involvement Management*. San Francisco: Jossey-Bass, 1986.

———. *Motivation in Work Organizations*. Monterey, Calif.: Brooks/Cole, 1973.

Lawler, E. E., and Cohen, S. G. "Designing Pay Systems for Teams." *ACA Journal* 1, no. 1 (Autumn 1992).

Lawler, E. E., and Mohrman, S. A. "Quality Circles After the Fad." *Harvard Business Review* (January–February 1985): 64–71.

Lee, C. "Beyond Teamwork." *Training* (June 1990): 25–32.

———. "Worker Harmony Makes NUMMI Work." *New York Times* (December 25, 1988): Sec. 3, p. 2.

Lewin, K. *Field Theory in Social Sciences*. New York: Harper, 1951.

Likert, R. *New Patterns of Management*. New York: McGraw-Hill, 1961.

Lorsch, J. W., and Lawrence, P. R., eds., *Managing Group and Intergroup Relations*. Homewood, Ill.: Dorsey, 1972.

Luft, J. *Group Processes: An Introduction to Group Dynamics*. 3d ed. Palo Alto, Calif.: Mayfield, 1984.

Manz, C. C., and Sims, H. P., Jr. "Leading Self-Managed Groups: A Conceptual Analysis of a Paradox." *Economic and Industrial Democracy* 7 (1986): 141–165.

———. *Superleadership*. New York: Prentice Hall, 1989.

Marrow, A. J. *Management by Participation*. New York: Harper, 1967.

Maslow, A. H. "A Theory of Human Motivation. *Psychological Review* 50 (1943): 370–396.

Mayo, E. *The Human Problems of an Industrial Civilization*. Cambridge, Mass.: Harvard University, 1933. Chapter 3.

McConnell, T. *Group Leadership for Self-Realization*. New York: Petrocelli, 1974.

McGregor, D. *The Human Side of Enterprise*. New York: McGraw-Hill, 1960, 1985.

———. *The Professional Manager*. New York: McGraw-Hill, 1967.

Merry, U., and Allerhand, M. E. *Developing Teams and Organizations*. Reading, Mass.: Addison-Wesley, 1977.

Miles, M. B. *Learning to Work in Groups*. 2d ed. New York: Teachers College Press, 1981.

Mills, T. M. "Changing Paradigms for Studying Human Groups." *Journal of Applied Behavioral Science* 15 (1979): 407.

Mohrman, A. M., Mohrman, S. A., and Cohen, S. "Human Resources Strategies for Lateral Integration in High Technology Settings." In L. Gomez-Mejia and M. Lawless, eds., *Human Resources Management Strategy in High Technology*. Greenwich, Conn.: JAI Press, 1992.

Mohrman, A. M., Mohrman, S. A., and Lawler, E. E. "The Performance Management of Teams." *Performance Measurement, Evaluation and Incentives*. Boston: Harvard Business School Press, 1992.

Moore, M. L. "Assess Organization Planning and Teamwork." *Journal of Applied Behavioral Science* 14 (1978): 479.

Moskal, B. S. "The Wizards of Buick City." *Industry Week* (May 7, 1990): 22–28.

Mower, J. C., and Wilemon, D. "Rewarding Technical Teamwork." *Research Technology Management* (September–October 1989): 24–29.

Nora, J. J., Rogers, C. R., and Stramy, R. J. *Transforming the Workplace*. Princeton, N.J.: Princeton Research Press, 1986.

Norman, C. A., and Zawacki, R. A. "Team Appraisals—Team Approach." *Personnel Journal* 70, no. 9 (September 1991): 101–104.

O'Dell, C. "Team Play, Team Pay—New Ways of Keeping Score." *Across the Board* (November 1989): 38–45.

Orsburn, J., Moran, L., Musselwhite, E., and Zenger, J. *Self-Directed Work Teams: The New American Challenge*. Homewood, Ill.: Business One Irwin, 1990.

Patinkin, M. "Gamble on Assembly Teams Pays Off." *Pittsburgh Press* (1987): B6–B7.

Patten, T. H., Jr. *Organizational Development Through Teambuilding*. New York: Wiley, 1981.

Patton, B. R., and Griffin, K. *Problem-Solving Group Interaction*. New York: Harper, 1973.

Pearce, J. A., III, and Ravlin, E. C. "The Design and Activation of Self-Regulating Workgroups." *Human Relations* 40 (1987): 33–37.

Peters, T. *Thriving on Chaos: Handbook for a Management Revolution*. New York: Knopf, 1987.

Quick, T. *Successful Team Building*. New York: AMACOM, 1992.

Ryan, K. D., and Oestreich, D. K. *Driving Fear Out of the Workplace*. San Francisco: Jossey-Bass, 1991.

Schein, E. H. *Organizational Culture and Leadership: A Dynamic View*. San Francisco: Jossey-Bass, 1985.

Scherer, J. J. "Can Team-Building Increase Productivity? Or How Can Something That Feels So Good Not Be Worthwhile?" *Group and Organizational Studies* 4 (1979): 335.

Scholtes, P. R. *The Team Handbook*. Madison, Wis.: Joiner, 1988.

Schonberger, R. J. *World Class Manufacturing Casebook: Implementing JIT and TQC*. New York: Free Press, 1987.

Semler, R. "Managing Without Managers." *Harvard Business Review* 89, no. 5 (September–October 1989): 76–84.

Sheridan, J. H. "America's Best Plants." *Industry Week* (October 1990): 27–44.

Sherwood, J. J. "Creating Work Cultures With Competitive Advantage." *Organization Dynamics* (Winter 1988): 5–27.

Sherwood, J. J., and Woodman, R. W. "Effects of Team Development Intervention: A Field Experiment." *Journal of Applied Behavioral Science* 16 (1980): 221–227.

Sims, H. P., Jr., and Dean, J. W., Jr. "Beyond Quality Circles: Self-Managing Teams." *Personnel* 62 (1985): 25–32.

Smith, K. K. *Groups in Conflict: Prisons in Disguise*. Dubuque, Iowa: Kendall-Hunt, 1982.

Smith, P. B., and Peterson, M. F. *Leadership, Organizations and Culture.* Beverly Hills, Calif.: Sage, 1988.

Taylor, F. W. *The Principles of Scientific Management.* New York: Harper, 1919.

Tregoe, B. B., and Kepner, C. H. *The Rational Manager.* New York: McGraw-Hill, 1965.

Trist, E. L., and Bamforth, K. W. "Some Social and Psychological Consequences of the Long-Wall Method of Coal Getting." *Human Relations* (1951): 3–38.

Tubbs, S. L. *A Systems Approach to Small Group Interaction.* New York: Random House, 1988.

Tuckman, B. W. "Development Sequence in Small Groups." *Psychological Bulletin* 63 (1965): 384–399.

Varney, G. H. *Building Productive Teams.* San Francisco: Jossey-Bass, 1990.

———. *Teambuilding: A Self-Directed Approach to Improving Work Teams.* Bowling Green, Ohio: Management Advisory Associates, 1985.

Vroom, V. H. *Work and Motivation.* New York: Wiley, 1964.

Walton, R. E. "From Control to Commitment in the Workplace." *Harvard Business Review* (November–December 1984): 172–182.

———. *Managing Conflict: Interpersonal Dialogue and Third-Party Roles.* 2d ed. Reading, Mass.: Addison-Wesley, 1987.

Waterman, R. H. *The Renewal Factor.* New York: Bantam, 1988.

Weisbord, M. R. *Productive Workplaces: Organizing and Managing for Dignity, Meaning, and Community.* San Francisco: Jossey-Bass, 1987.

Wellins, R. S., Byham, W. C., and Wilson, J. M. *Empowered Teams.* San Francisco: Jossey-Bass, 1991.

Wesner, M., and Egan, C. "Self-Managed Teams in Operator Services." Paper presented at International Conference on Self-Managed Work Teams, Denton, Tex., September 1990.

Woodcock, M., and Francis, D. *Organization Development Through Teambuilding.* Aldershot, England: Gower, 1981.

Wysocki, L. "Implementation of Self-Managed Teams Within a Non-Union Manufacturing Facility." Paper presented at International Conference on Self-Managed Work Teams, Denton, Tex., September 1990.

Zenger, J. J., and Miller, D. E. "Building Effective Teams." *Personnel* 51 (1974): 20–29.

Zuboff, S. *In the Age of the Smart Machine.* New York: Basic, 1988.

Index

[Page numbers indicating definitions or explanations of certain important terms are boldfaced. Page numbers indicating illustrations are in italics.]